Coding Buddies

A Simple Journey into Python

MAK LUI

Copyright © 2023 Mak Lui
All rights reserved
ISBN: 9798399999401

Only you can control your future
The first step is as good as half over

Content

1 Chapter 1 Introduction 1
    1.1   Welcome to Coding Buddies 2
    1.2   Overview of Python and its Popularity 3
    1.3   Benefits of learning Python 4
2 Chapter 2 Getting Started with Python 5
    2.1   Install Python 6
    2.2   Install Visual Studio Code 12
    2.3   Install Python Extension for Visual Studio Code 22
    2.4   Create The "Hello World" Program 28
3 Chapter 3 Variables and Data Types 38
    3.1   Understanding Variables and Purpose 39
    3.2   Rules of the Variables 45
    3.3   Exploring Different Data Types 46
    3.4   Understanding Lists 49
4 Chapter 4 Comments and Operators 51
    4.1   Understanding Comments 52
    4.2   Understanding Operators 54
    4.3   Arithmetic Operators 55
    4.4   Assignment Operators 59
    4.5   Comparison Operators 64
    4.6   Logical Operators 70
    4.7   Identity Operators 75
    4.8   Membership Operators 78
5 Chapter 5 Control Flow and Decision Making 80

	5.1	Understanding the Control Flow	81
	5.2	Conditional	82
	5.3	Looping	87
6	Chapter 6 Functions and Modules		92
	6.1	Understanding Functions	93
	6.2	Exploring Common Functions	95
	6.3	Creating New Functions	109
	6.4	Organizing With Modules	112
	6.5	Exploring Built-in Modules	114
7	Chapter 7 External Modules		117
	7.1	Understanding External Module	118
	7.2	PIP Install	119
	7.3	Using External Module	121
8	The Last Tips		132
9	Appendix		134
	9.1	ASCII Code Table	135
	9.2	Format Option	136

ACKNOWLEDGMENTS

I am grateful to all of those with whom I have had the pleasure to work during this project.

Truong Nhat Vy Nguyen
Stephen Chen

Chapter 1
Introduction

1 Introduction

1.1 Welcome to Coding Buddies

Welcome to Coding Buddies, your friendly companions on the path to a successful coding career! We're here to make learning Python a breeze, with simple explanations and bite-sized lessons that won't overwhelm you.

Whether you're a total beginner or just starting to explore the world of programming, we've got your back. Our goal is to help you succeed in your dream career by providing the support and guidance you need.

So, get ready to dive into Python with us and unlock the exciting possibilities that coding has to offer. Let's keep it short, fast, and easy as we embark on this exciting journey together!

This book aims to get you started and give you the skills that you needed, you will know how to find updated and advanced technology by yourself.

All the sample code can be downloaded here.
https://sites.google.com/view/coding-buddies

1 Introduction

1.2 Overview of Python and its Popularity

Python, the beloved programming language, has an intriguing history that has contributed to its immense popularity today. Created by Guido van Rossum and first released in 1991, Python was designed with a focus on simplicity and readability. Its name was inspired by the British comedy group Monty Python, showcasing the language's fun and whimsical nature. Over the years, Python's popularity grew steadily, thanks to its user-friendly syntax, vast library ecosystem, and strong community support.

Today, Python is widely used in various industries and has become the go-to language for tasks ranging from web development to scientific computing and machine learning. Its growth can be attributed to its versatility, ease of use, and the passionate community that continually contributes to its development. Python's journey from a pet project to a powerful programming language has left an indelible mark on the world of coding, making it an incredible tool for beginners and experienced developers.

1 Introduction

1.3 Benefits of learning Python

Welcome to the world of Python, where coding dreams come to life! With its simplicity and versatility, Python has become one of the most popular programming languages worldwide. Here's what makes Python special.

Friendly Approachable

Python's user-friendly syntax makes it easy to read and write, perfect for beginners.

Community Support

Join a thriving community of Python enthusiasts who are always ready to help and share knowledge.

Versatile Applications

Python can be used for web development, data analysis, machine learning, and much more.

Extensive Library

Take advantage of a rich collection of pre-built libraries and tools to supercharge your projects.

Whether you aspire to build websites, analyze data, or create cutting-edge applications, Python is your passport to success. Let's embark on this exciting journey together and unlock the endless possibilities of Python programming!

Chapter 2
Getting Started with Python

2 Getting Started with Python

2.1 Install Python

Ready to embark on your Python coding adventure? Great! Let's start by getting Python up and running on your computer. Don't worry, the installation process is a breeze, and we're here to guide you every step of the way.

Installing Python is a straightforward process that varies slightly depending on your operating system. Python is available for Windows, macOS, and Linux, ensuring compatibility across platforms.

2 Getting Started with Python

Step 1

Go to https://www.python.org/, and click "Downloads" from the menu.

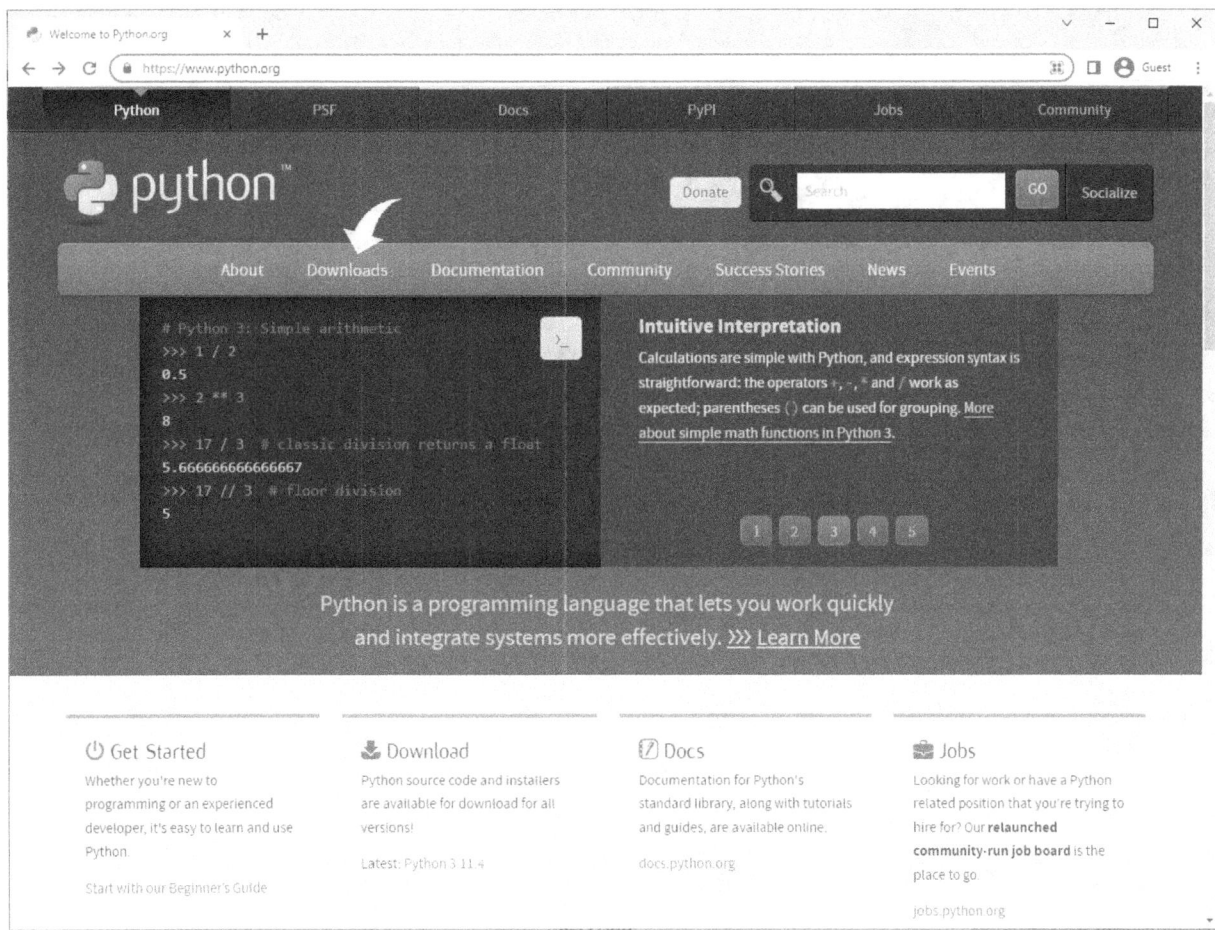

Step 2

Click the download button below, the program will download automatically.

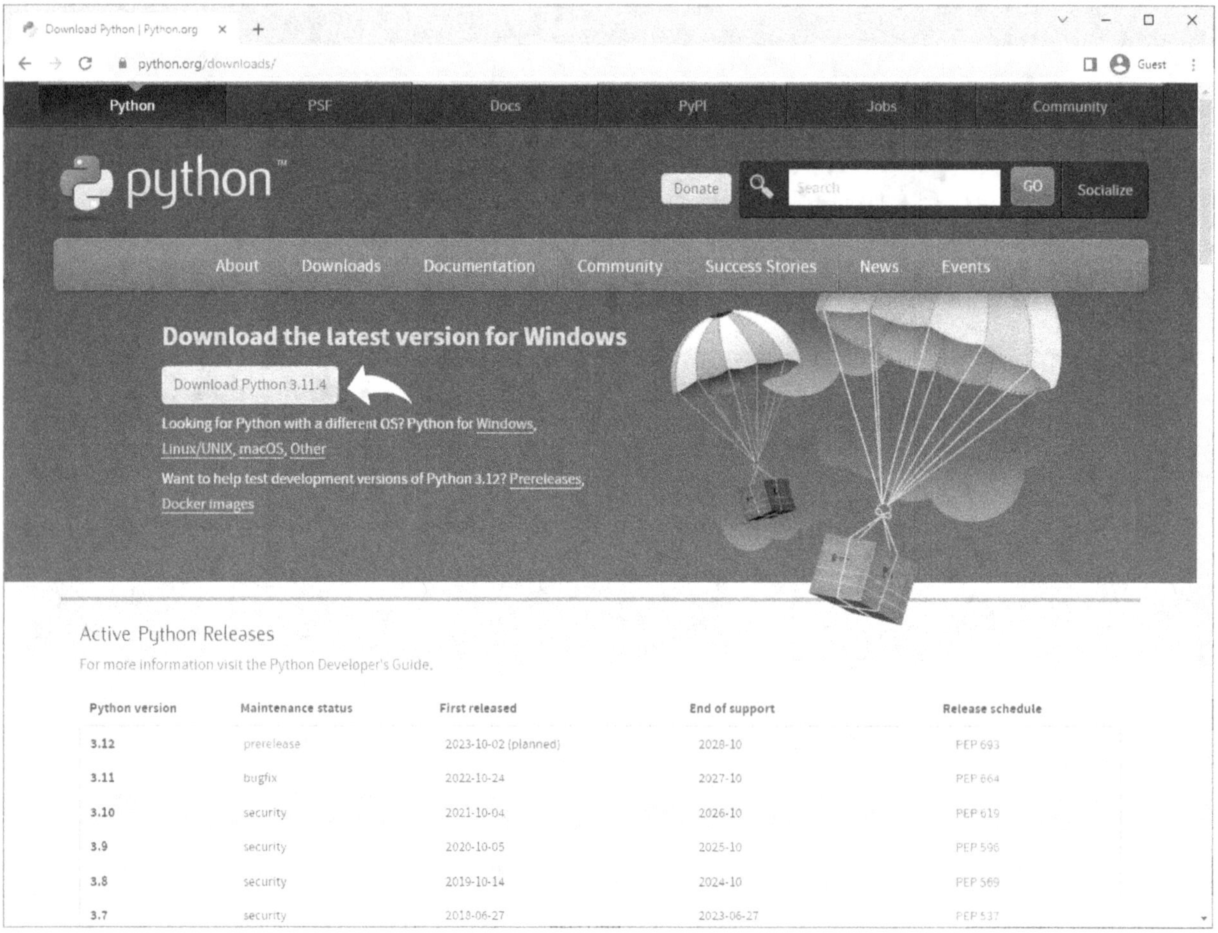

> Notes
> - It will choose the correct version for your system.
> - Different versions may have some minor differences, but the basic flow is the same.
> - Windows is used for this sample.

Step 3

Go to the download folder, mouse right-click on the file, and click "Run as administrator".

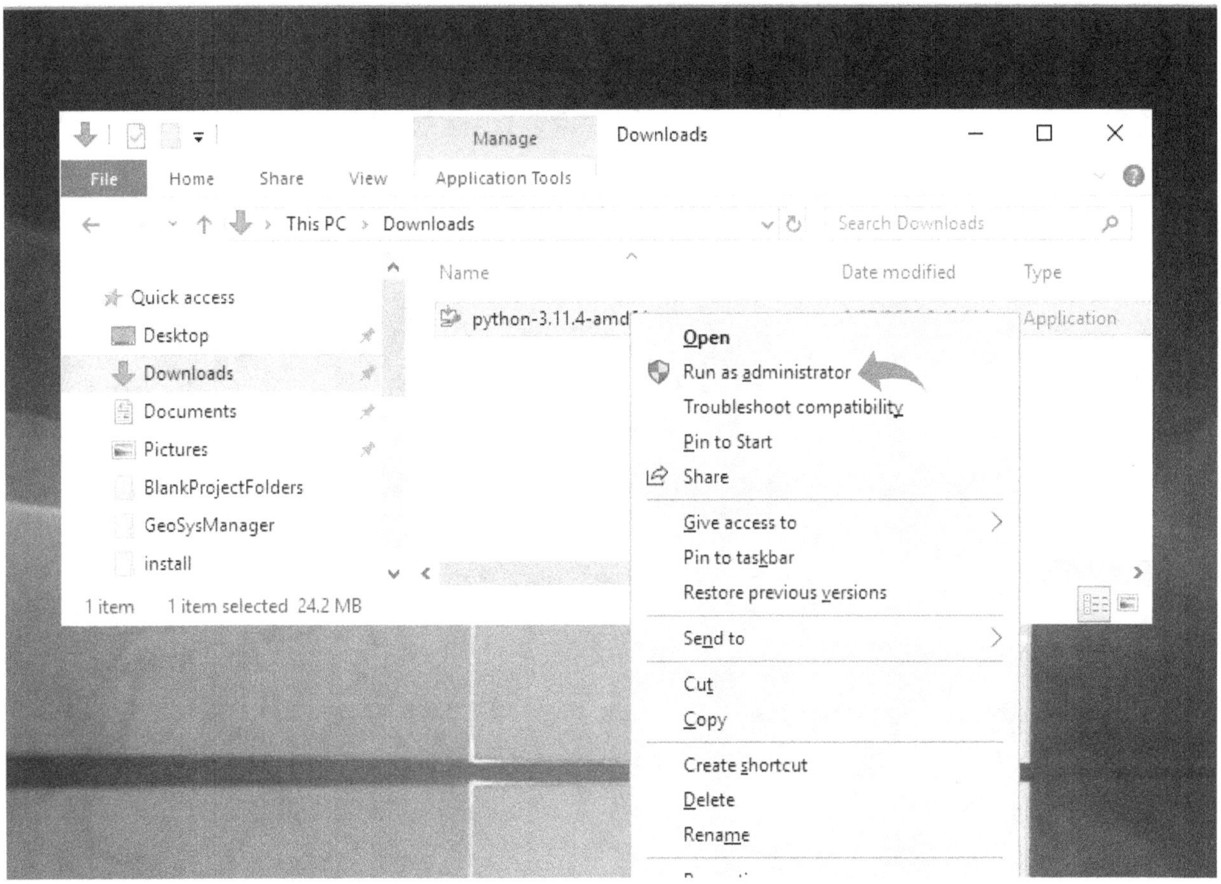

Notes

- It needs the administrator's right to do the configuration.
- Accept the run with administrator right if there has a popup for that.

2 Getting Started with Python

Step 4

Check the "Add python.exe to PATH" and click "Install Now".

 Notes
- Add pyhon.exe to PATH, let the installer do the setting for you.

Step 5

Click "Close" to finish the setup.

2.2 Install Visual Studio Code

Visual Studio Code, commonly called VS Code, is a versatile and user-friendly code editor offering a delightful Integrated Development Environment (IDE) experience. Its intuitive interface and wide range of features make it a beloved tool for developers worldwide. Here's a short overview of this friendly coding companion:

User-Friendly interface

A modern interface that makes coding a joyous experience.

Cross-Platform Support

VS Code has your back whether you're using Windows, macOS, or Linux.

Extensibility

VS Code boasts a vibrant ecosystem of extensions that enhance your coding capabilities.

Active Community

Join a welcoming and active community of developers who are always ready to assist.

2 Getting Started with Python

Step 1

Go to https://code.visualstudio.com/, and click the download button, the program will download automatically.

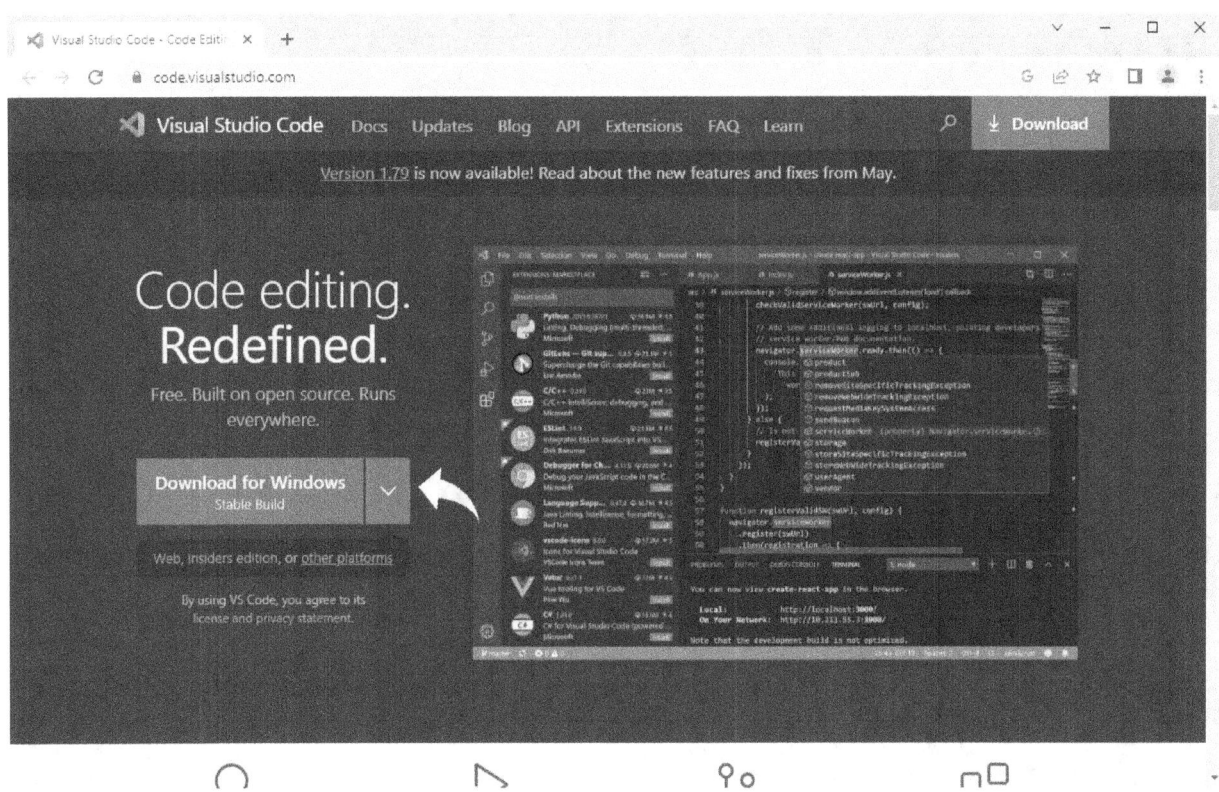

 Notes

- It will choose the correct version for your system.
- Different versions may have some minor differences, but the basic flow is the same.
- Windows is used for this sample.

2 Getting Started with Python

Step 2

Go to the download folder, mouse right-click on the file, and click "Run as administrator".

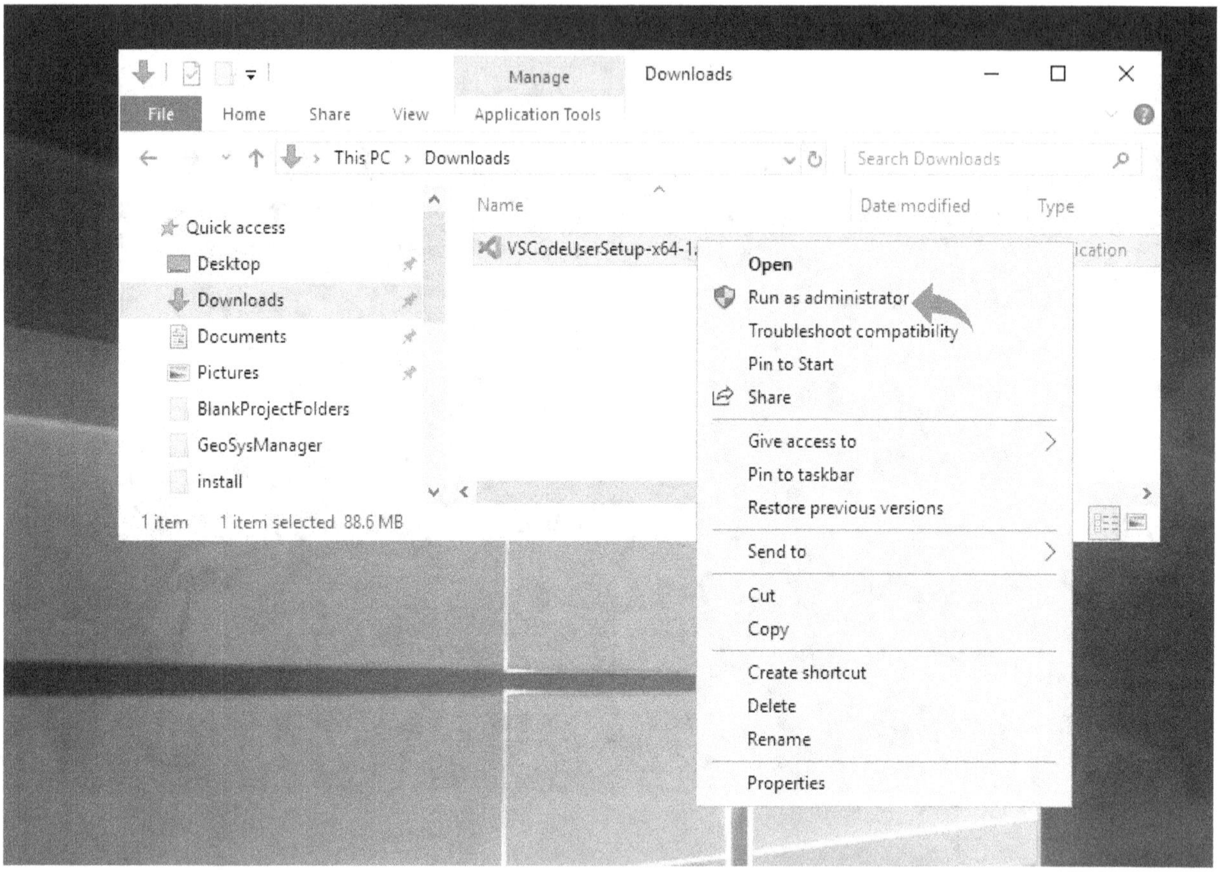

 Notes
- It needs the administrator's right to do the configuration.

Step 3

Accept the agreement and click next.

Setup - Microsoft Visual Studio Code (User)

License Agreement
Please read the following important information before continuing.

Please read the following License Agreement. You must accept the terms of this agreement before continuing with the installation.

This license applies to the Visual Studio Code product. Source Code for Visual Studio Code is available at https://github.com/Microsoft/vscode under the MIT license agreement at https://github.com/microsoft/vscode/blob/main/LICENSE.txt. Additional license information can be found in our FAQ at https://code.visualstudio.com/docs/supporting/faq.

MICROSOFT SOFTWARE LICENSE TERMS

MICROSOFT VISUAL STUDIO CODE

● I accept the agreement
○ I do not accept the agreement

Next >   Cancel

2 Getting Started with Python

Step 4

Keep the default setting and click next.

 Setup - Microsoft Visual Studio Code (User) — □ ×

Select Destination Location
Where should Visual Studio Code be installed?

Setup will install Visual Studio Code into the following folder.

To continue, click Next. If you would like to select a different folder, click Browse.

C:\Users\test\AppData\Local\Programs\Microsoft VS Code   Browse...

At least 343.2 MB of free disk space is required.

< Back   Next >   Cancel

2 Getting Started with Python

Step 5

Keep the default setting and click next.

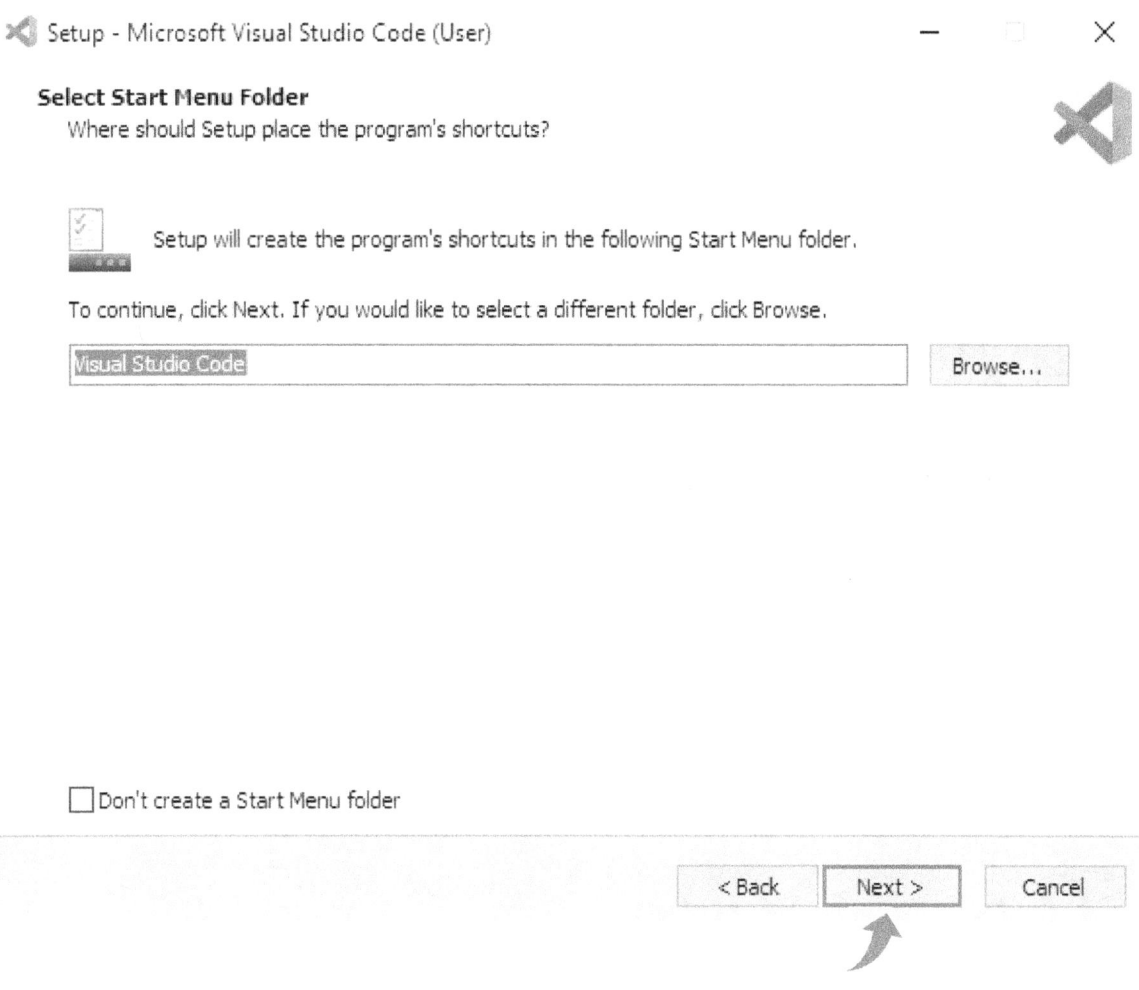

2 Getting Started with Python

Step 6

Check the "Create a desktop icon", and click next.

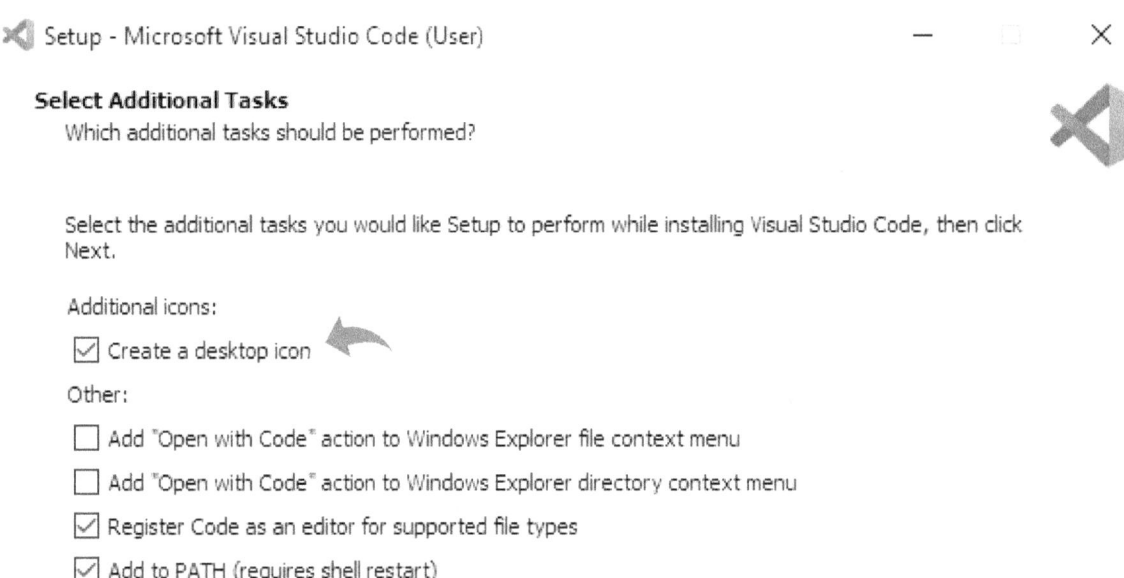

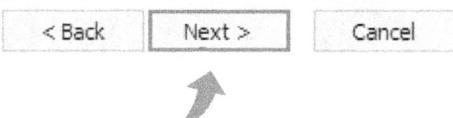

 Notes
- Create the desktop icon is easier for beginners to start VS code.

2 Getting Started with Python

Step 7

Click install.

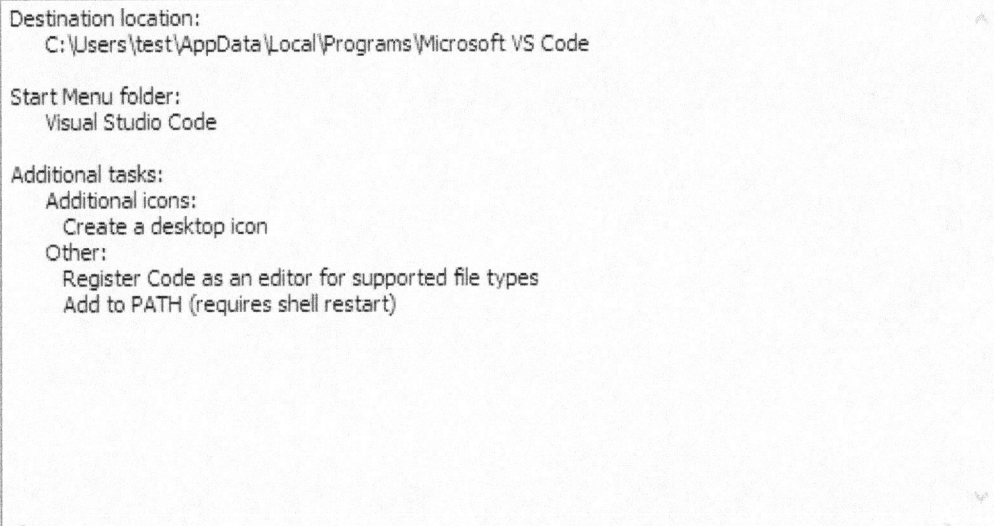

Step 8

Click finish.

2 Getting Started with Python

Step 9

Installation is done if you see this welcome page, you can choose any themes you like, light modern will be chosen for this sample.

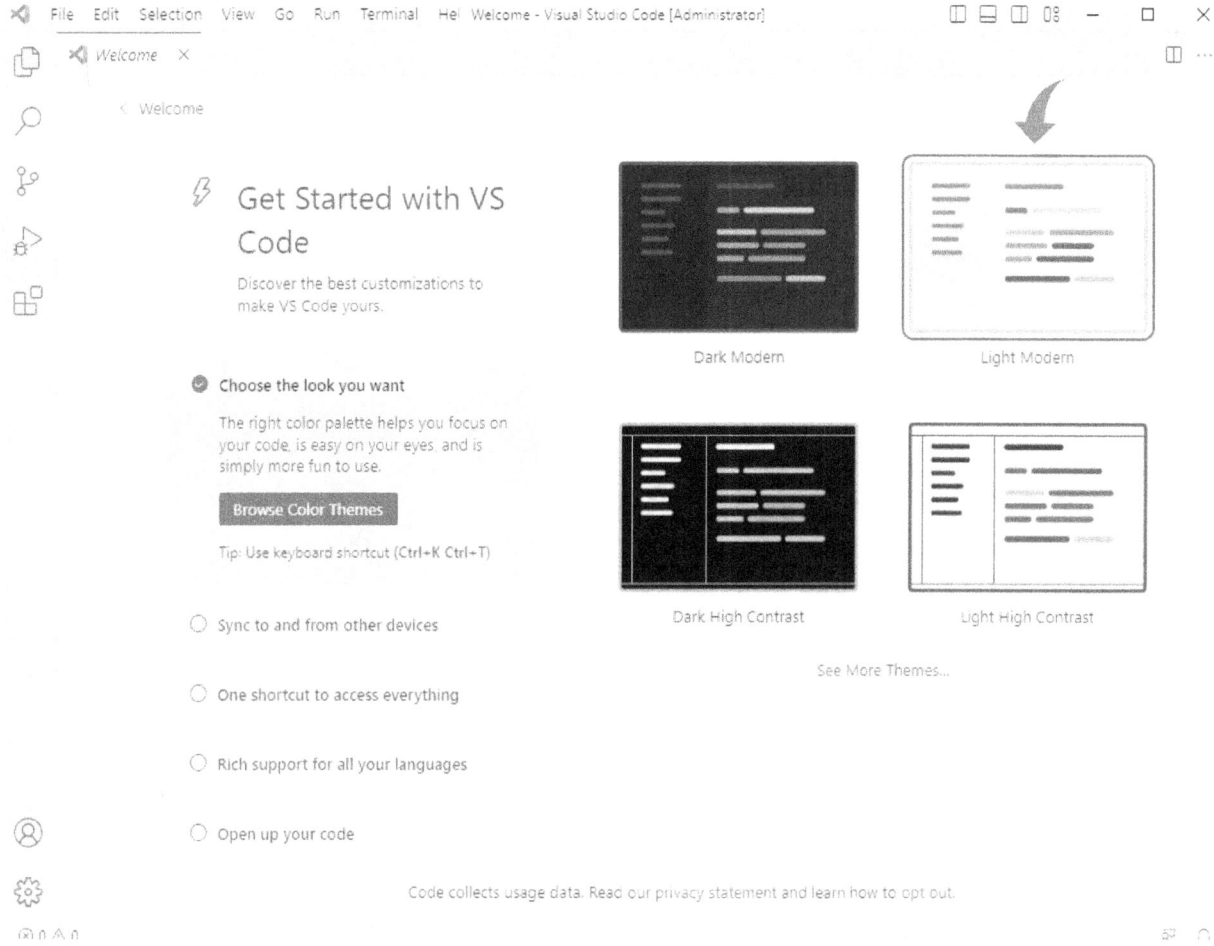

2.3 Install Python Extension for Visual Studio Code

The Python Extension for Visual Studio Code is a game-changer for Python developers, providing a seamless and delightful coding experience within the popular code editor. Designed specifically for Python, this extension brings many features and functionalities that empower you to easily write, debug, and explore Python code.

2 Getting Started with Python

Step 1

Click the extension icon.

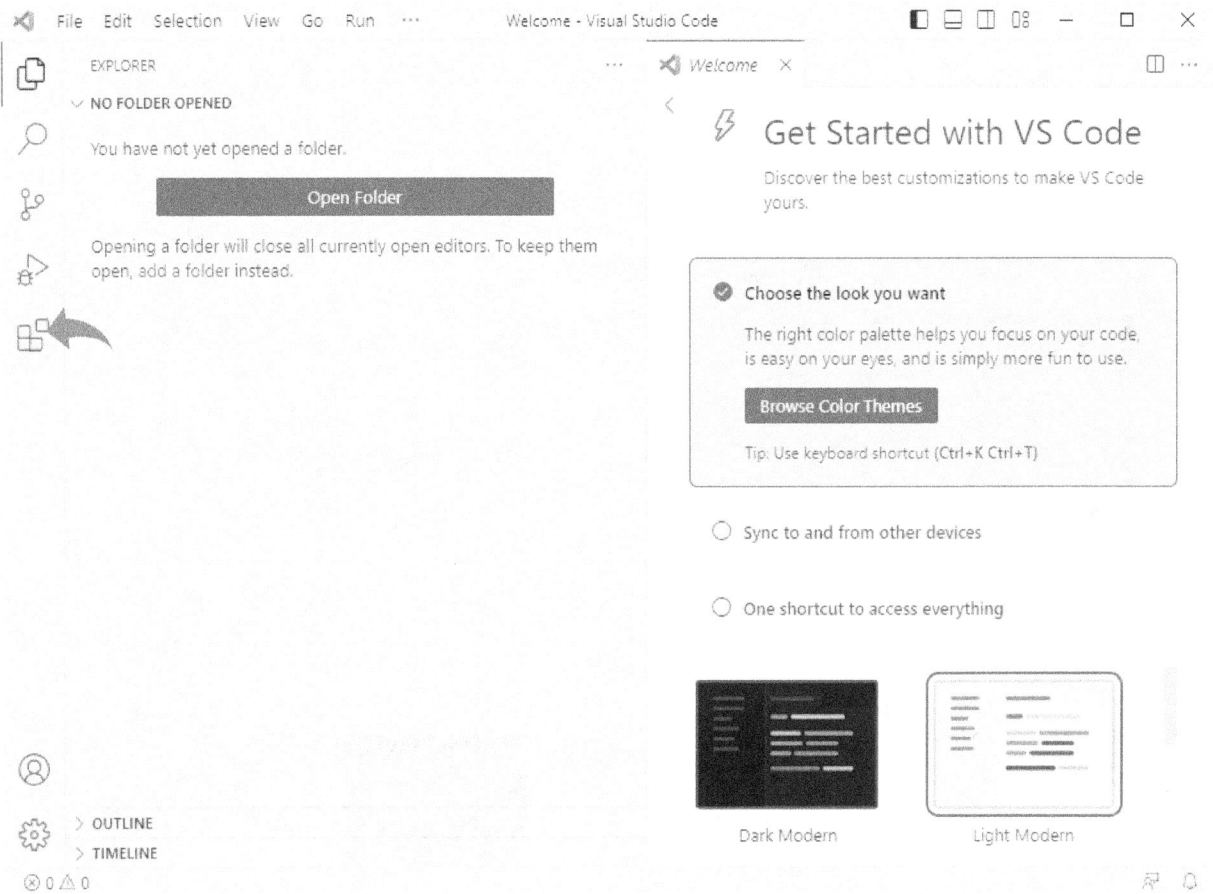

2 Getting Started with Python

Step 2

Enter "python" in the extensions marketplace textbox, and the "Python" will show, click the "Install" button.

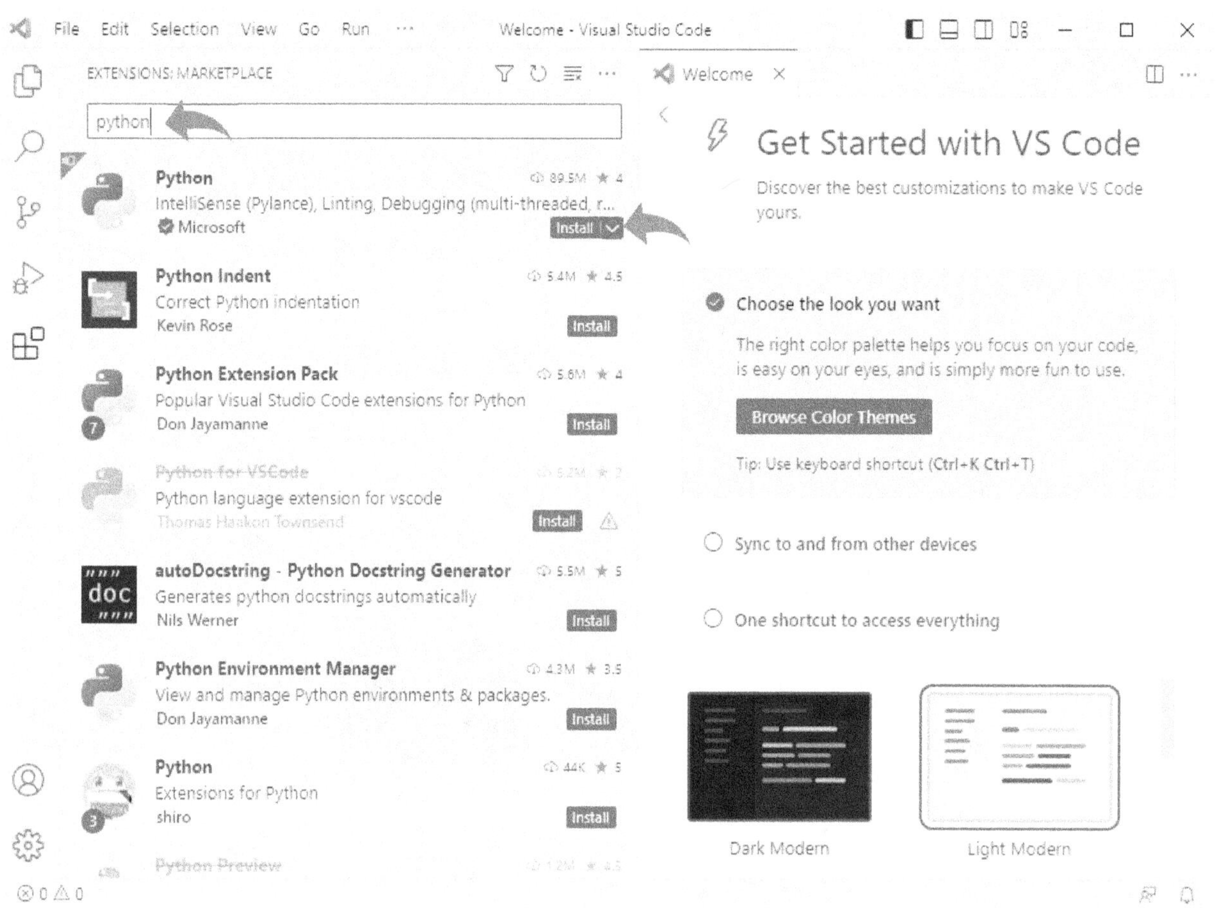

> **Notes**
> - Those with the blue tick are the official ones.

2 Getting Started with Python

Step 3

After the loading is done, you will see the "Select Python Interpreter" button, click it.

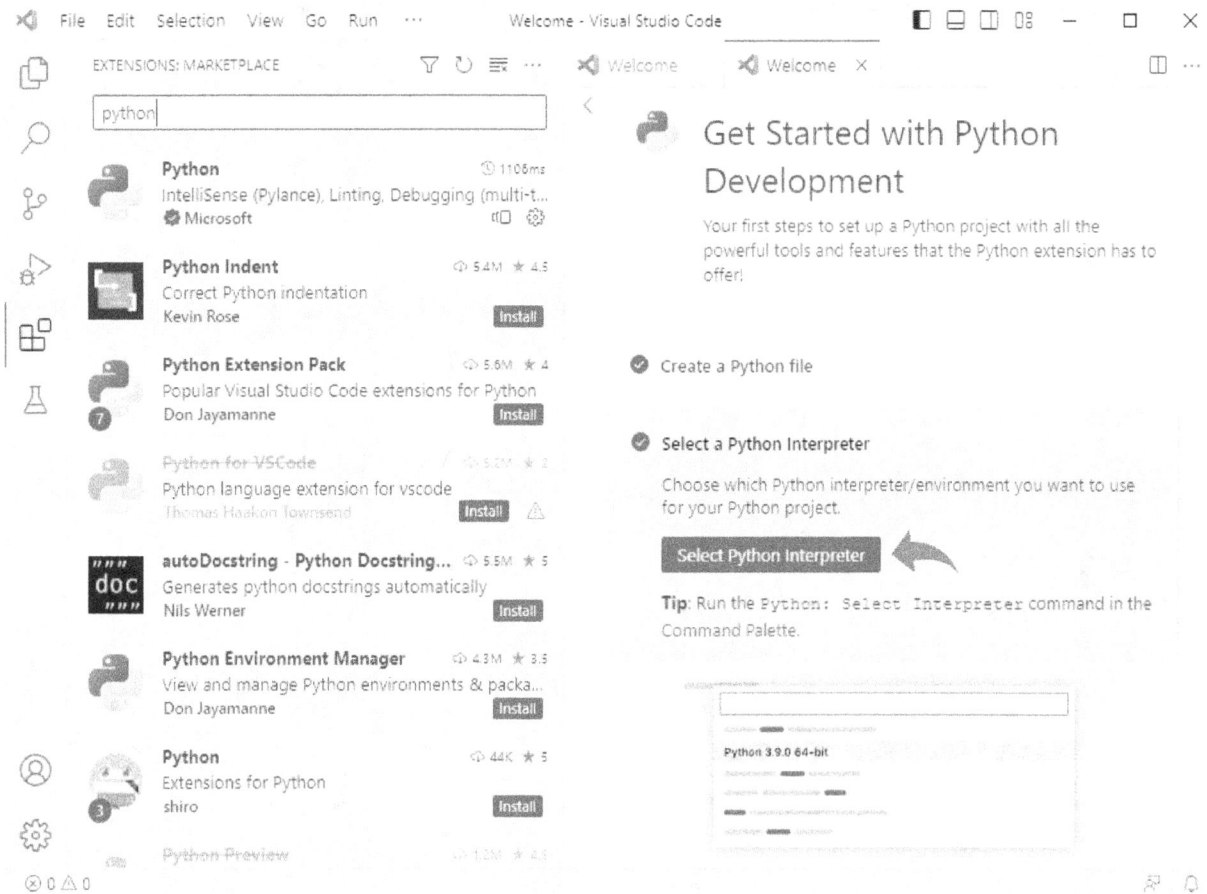

Step 4

Select the recommended one.

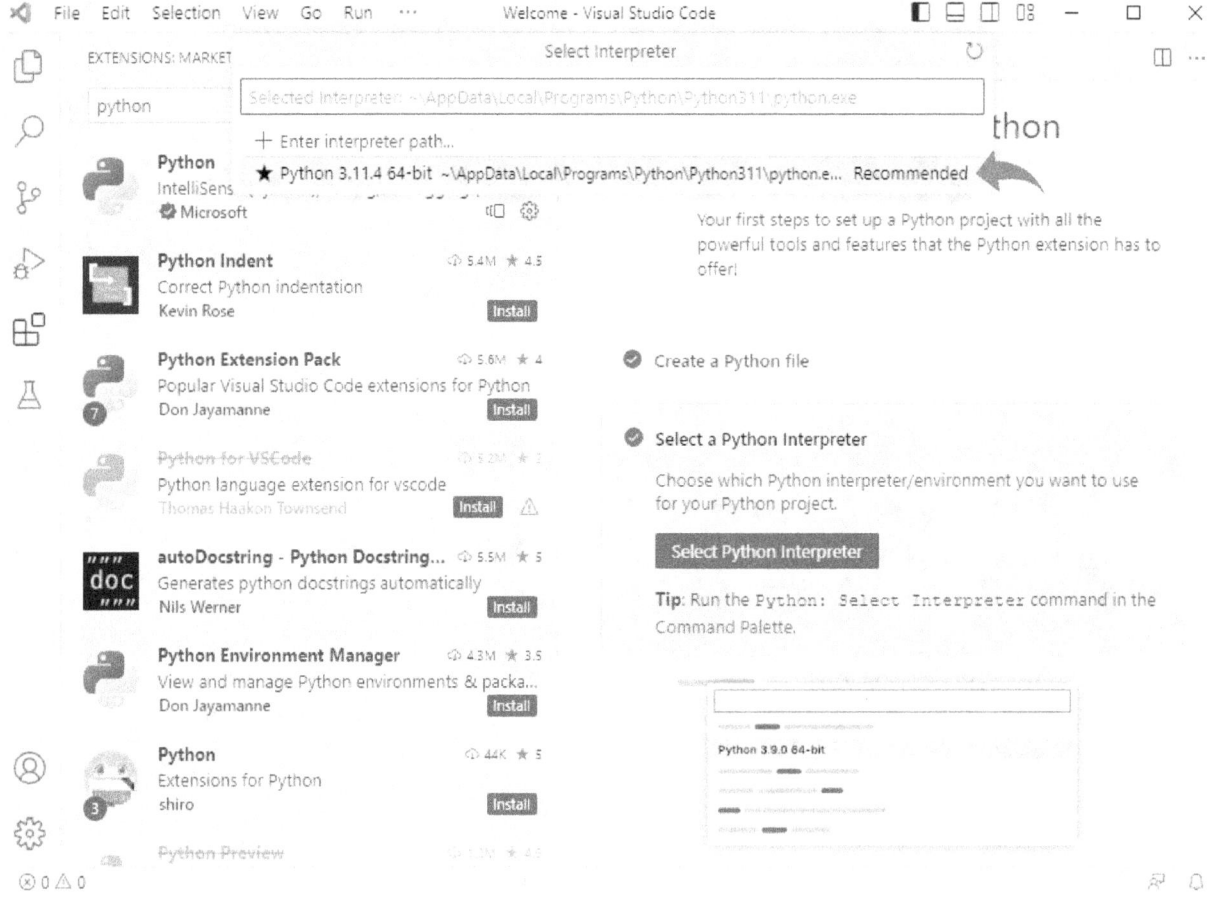

Step 5

Setup is done, you can click "X" to close the tab.

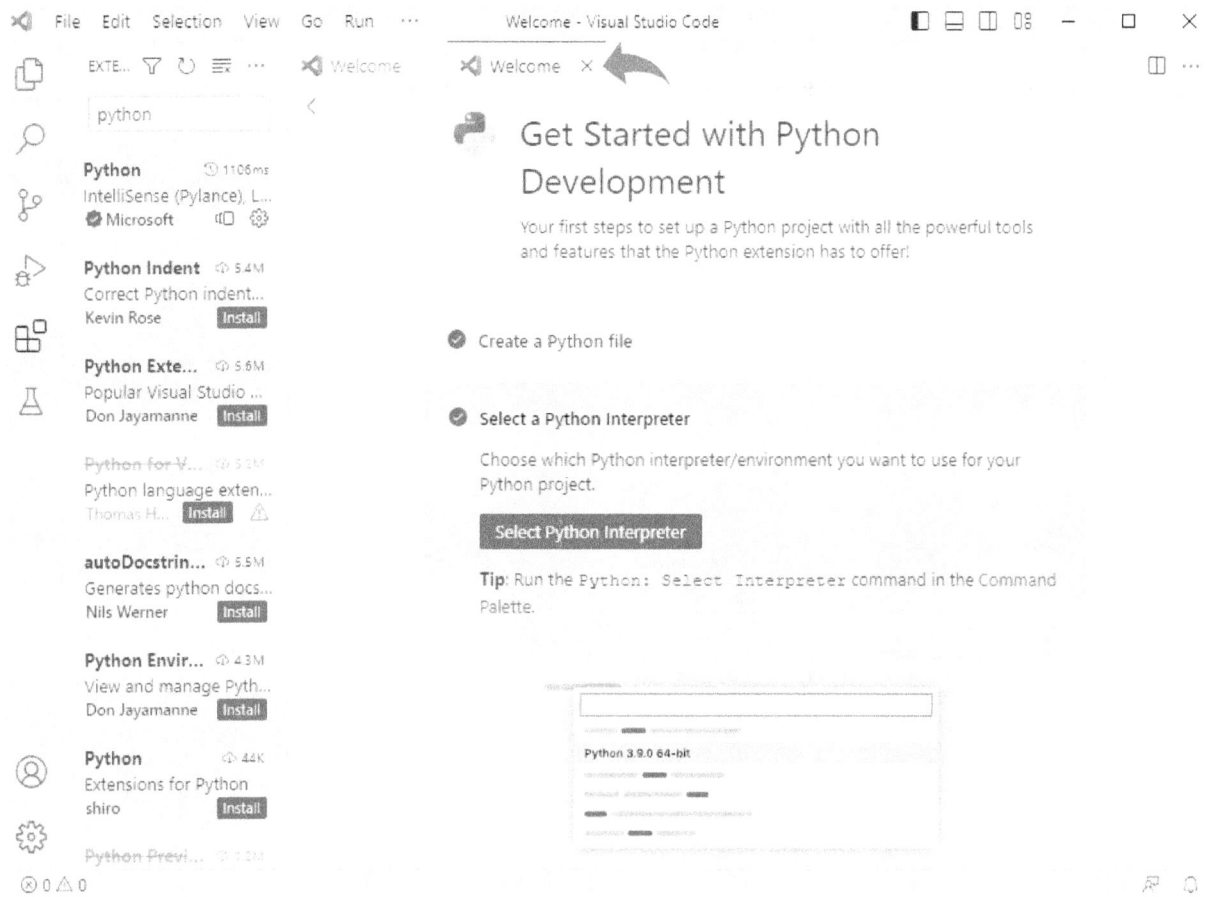

2.4 Create The "Hello World" Program

The "Hello World" program holds a special place in the hearts of programmers, it's where the coding journey begins, and it will be your first Python program.

2 Getting Started with Python

Step 1

Select "File" from the VS code menu, then click "New File".

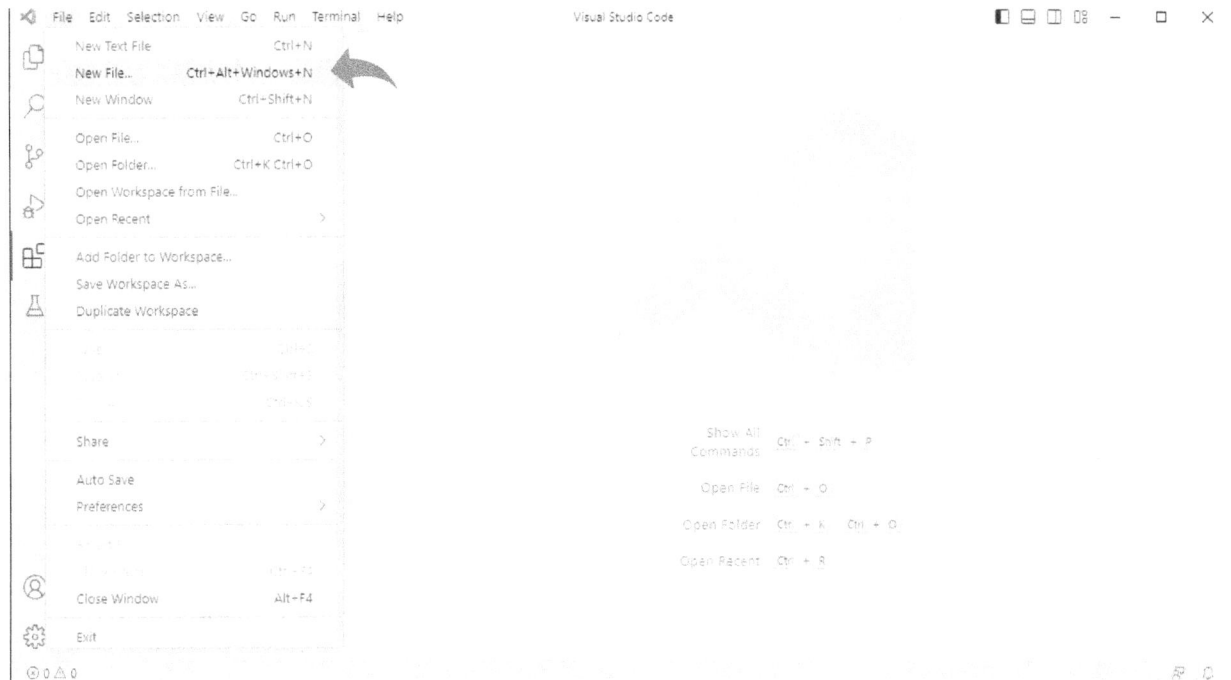

 Notes
- You can think of VS code as a text editor, you can also click "Open File" to open an existing file.

2 Getting Started with Python

Step 2

Click "Python File".

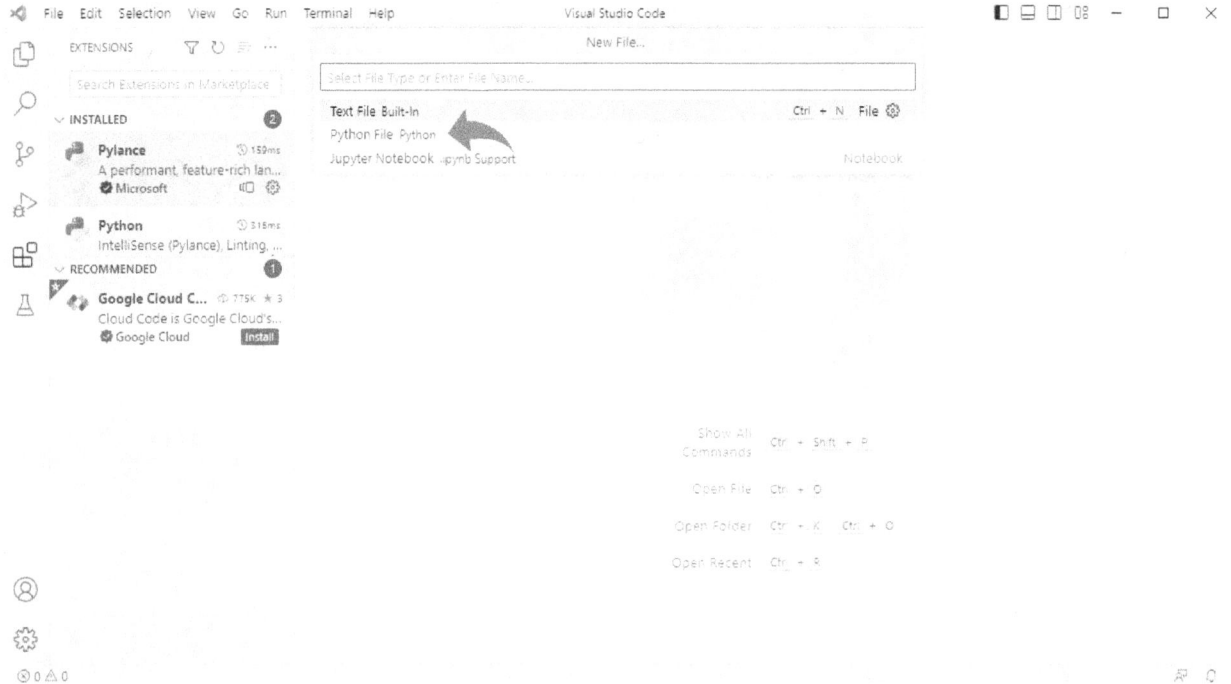

Here will be the workplace for your program code.

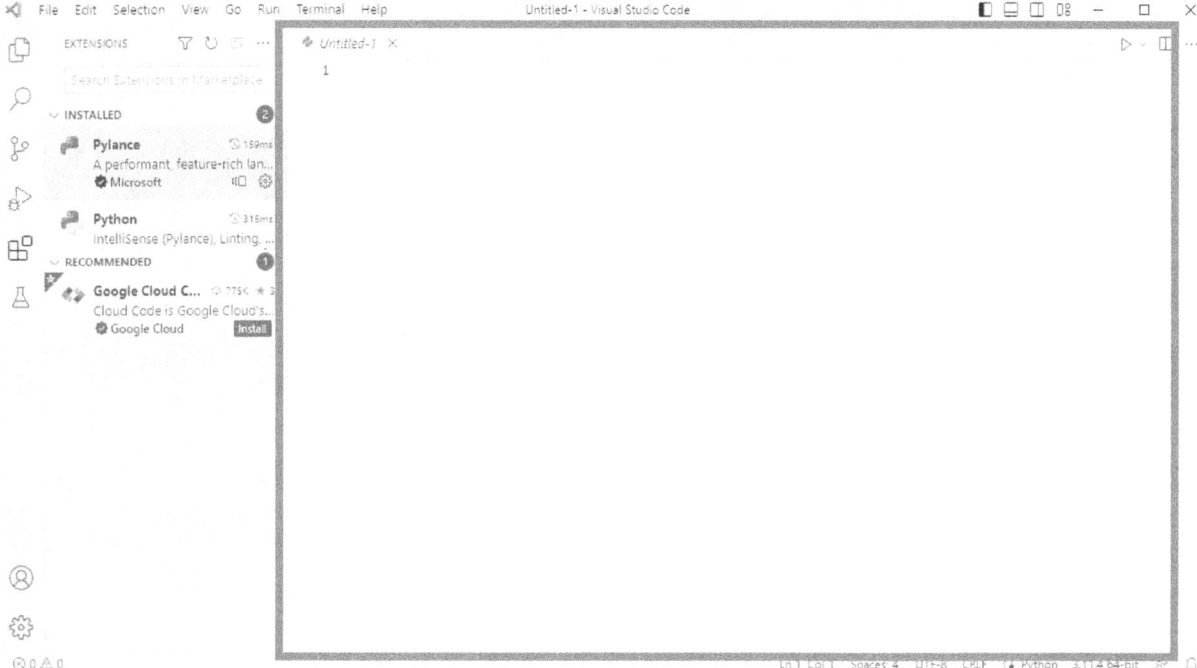

Step 3

Enter the code below in the workplace.

P_02_04_001.py

```
print("Hello World")
```

Here is what it looks like.

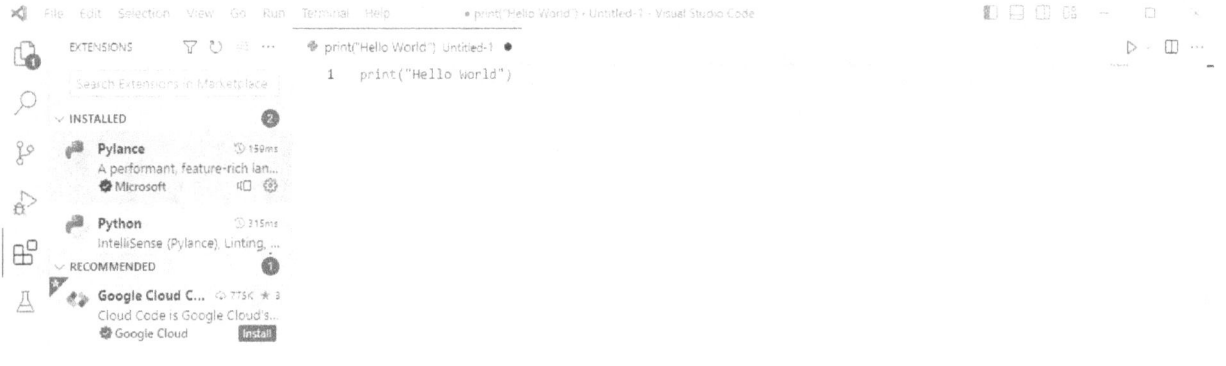

> Notes
> - For each line of the code, don't put any space before it, the space is used to present different levels of the program which will explain later on.

2 Getting Started with Python

Step 4

Click "File" from the menu, and Click "Save".

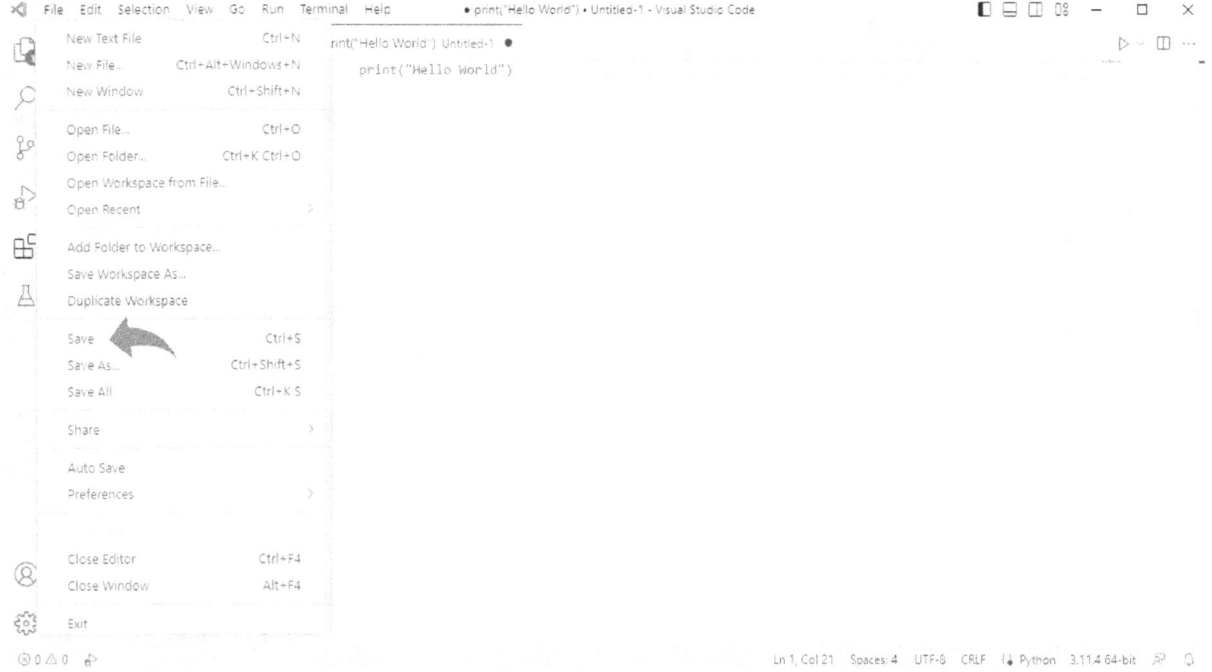

 **Notes**
- You must save the file first before you run it.

2 Getting Started with Python

Step 5

Select the location you like, enter the file name, then click "Save".

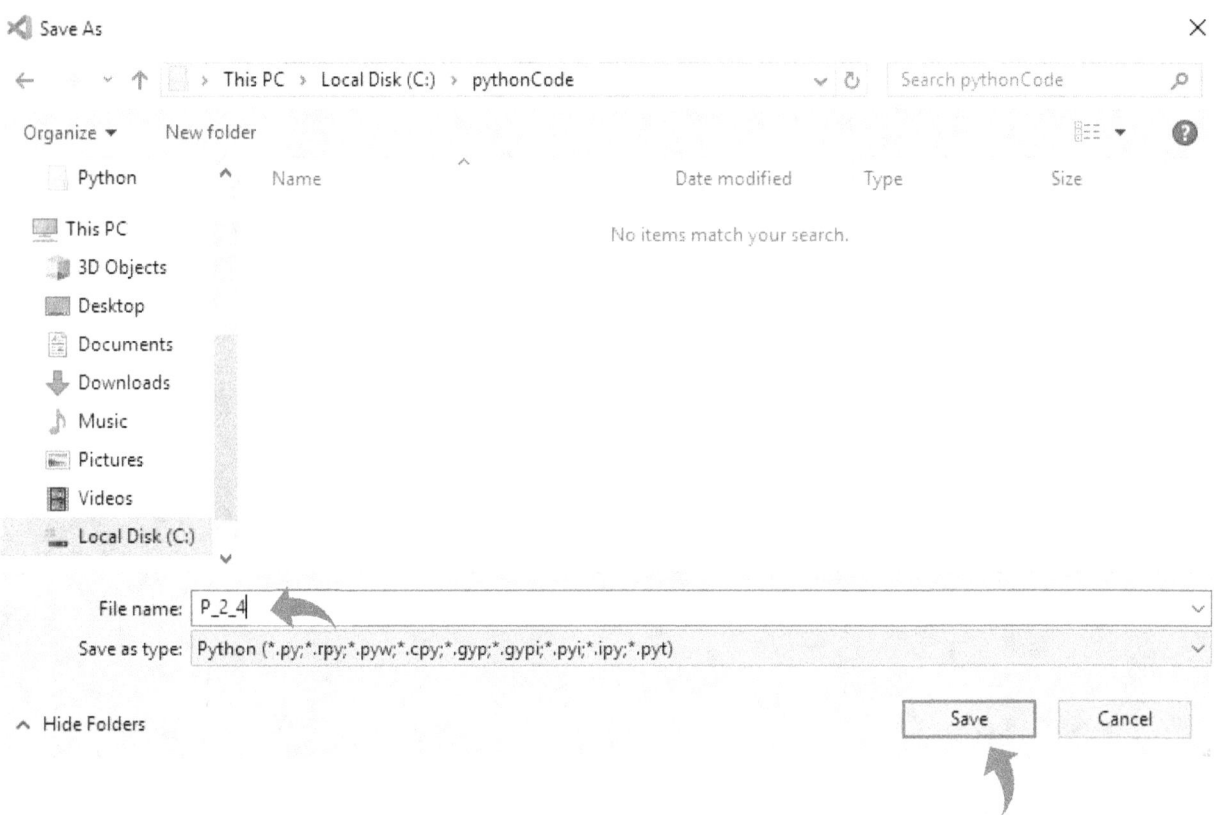

2 Getting Started with Python

Step 6

Click "Run" from the menu and Click "Start Debugging".

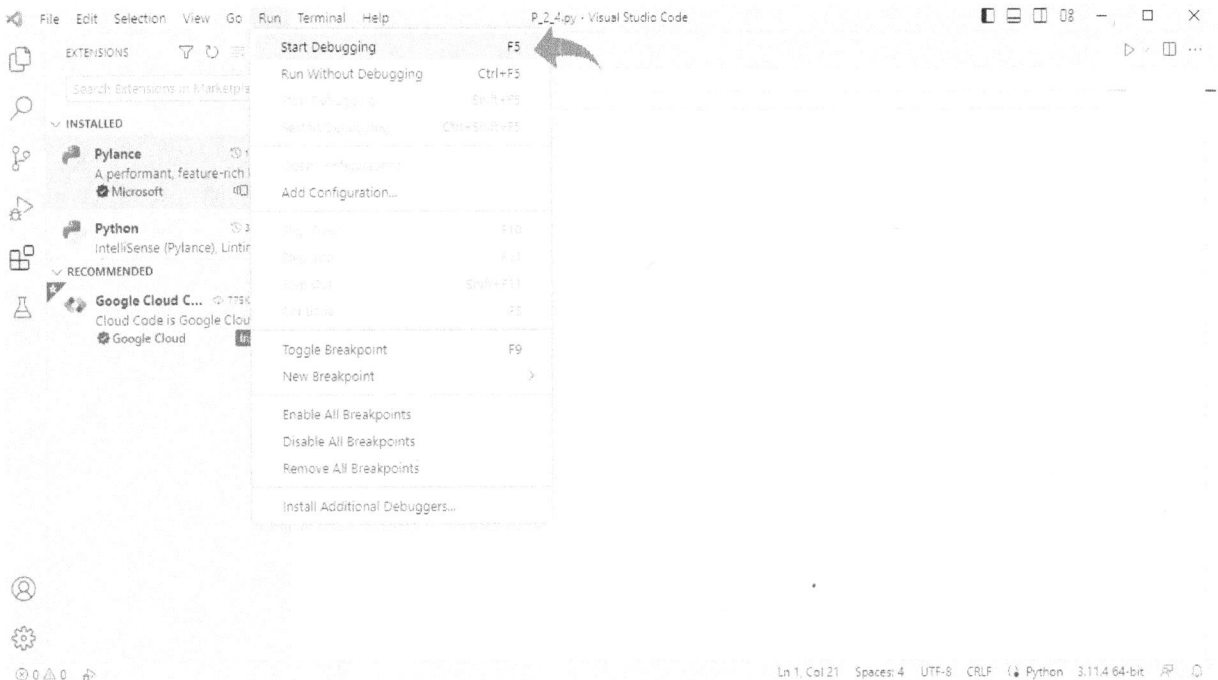

 Notes
- You can also use the "F5" key on the keyboard.

2 Getting Started with Python

Step 7

Select "Python file".

Select a debug configuration

Debug Configuration

Python File Debug the currently active Python file
Module Debug a Python module by invoking it with '-m'
Remote Attach Attach to a remote debug server
Attach using Process ID Attach to a local process
Django Launch and debug a Django web application
FastAPI Launch and debug a FastAPI web application
Flask Launch and debug a Flask web application
Pyramid Launch and debug a Pyramid web application

 Notes
- This box will not show every time.

2 Getting Started with Python

This area is the output from your program, if you can see the "Hello World" in it, that means the setup is done and Python works.

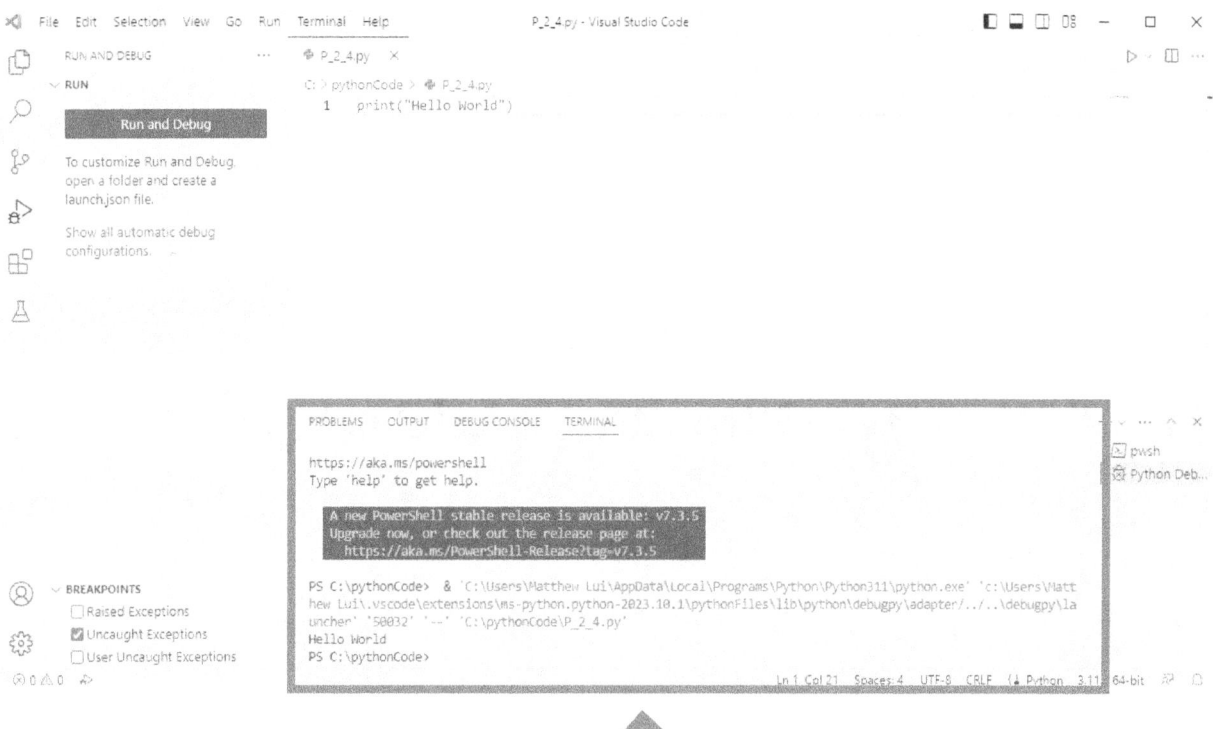

Chapter 3
Variables and Data Types

3 Variables and Data Types

3.1 Understanding Variables and Purpose

Hey there, coding adventurer! Let's dive into the fascinating world of variables and data types. Think of variables as these awesome containers that can hold all sorts of valuable information. They're like magical boxes where you can store and manipulate data within your program. Ready to understand how they work? Here are some friendly ideas to help explain variables and their exciting purpose.

You can imagine that the variables are boxes, each box has its value that can be assigned and changed.

For example, there is a variable called "Number of apples", at the beginning, it does don't have any value.

Number of apples

Then you can give it a value, let's say 5.

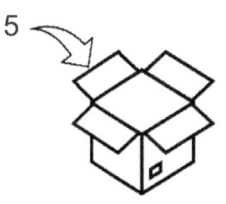

Number of apples

3 Variables and Data Types

So, from now on, the "Number of apples" will be 5.

Number of apples

If the "Number of apples" changes the other day, let's say 8, we can assign another value.

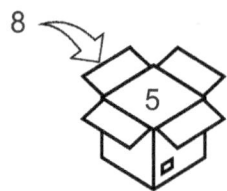

Number of apples

So, from now on, the "Number of apples" will be 8.

Number of apples

So, if we want to know the price for those apples, we can do "Number of apples" multiples $2, and we don't have to change the code every day.

Number of apples

> Notes
> - We will use variables a lot in programs since value will change but the code will not.

3 Variables and Data Types

It is what looks like in the code, "NumberOfApples" and "PriceOfApples" are the variables.

P_03_01_001.py

```
NumberOfApples = 5
NumberOfApples = 8
PriceOfApples = NumberOfApples * 2
```

It is what looks like in the VS code.

3 Variables and Data Types

Explanation

`NumberOfApples = 5`

> Assign variable "NumberOfApples" with a value 5.
>
> `NumberOfApples = 5`

`NumberOfApples = 8`

> Give a new value 8 to variable "NumberOfApples".
>
> `NumberOfApples = 8`

`PriceOfApples = NumberOfApples * 2`

> It will have 2 steps here.
>
> 1. Calculate the value "NumberOfApples * 2"
>
> `PriceOfApples = NumberOfApples * 2`
>
> ⇓
>
> `PriceOfApples = 16`
>
> 2. Assign variable "PriceOfApples" with a value 16
>
> `PriceOfApples = 16`

3 Variables and Data Types

However, if you want to know the value in the variable "PriceOfApples", you can a function called "print" to output the value to the terminal, here is the sample.

P_03_01_002.py

```
NumberOfApples = 5
NumberOfApples = 8
PriceOfApples = NumberOfApples * 2
print(PriceOfApples)
```

You will see the output after the run.

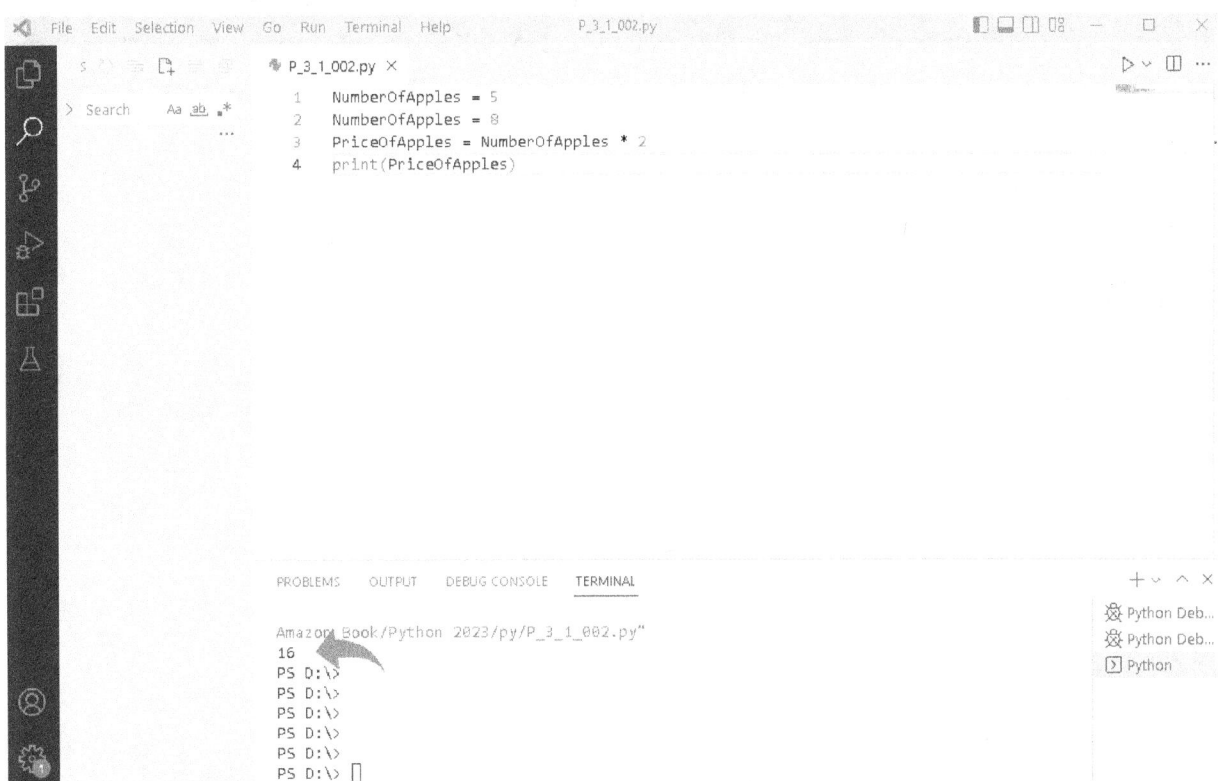

3 Variables and Data Types

Explanation

The function print will output inside the ( ), so the value of "PriceOfApples" will be outputted.

Naming the Variable

It is a good habit to name the variables with meaningful words, it can greatly increase the readability, and make debugging much easier, you can capitalize the first letter.

Good naming sample	Bad naming sample
PriceOfApple NameOfBook IsOnSales	Var1 Int1 Sales123

 Notes
- There has a lot of functions in Python, we will get into those later.
- Reminded that Python is case sensitive, so "Print" is not same as "print", "PriceOfApples" is not same as "priceOfApples"
- The value of a variable is "None" before it assigns any value.

3 Variables and Data Types

3.2 Rules of the Variables

Here are some rules for the name of the variables.

- They are case-sensitive.
- You can use uppercase and lowercase letters like (A-Z, a-z),
- You can use digits, like (0-9).
- You can use the underscore character which is (_).
- The first character cannot be a digit.

Valid variables sample

```
NumberOfApples
numberOfApples
number_Of_Apples
number_of_apples
_numberOfApples
```

Invalid variables sample

```
Number Of Apples
123numberOfApples
numberOfApples!
numberOf(Apples)
number.Of.Apples
```

3 Variables and Data Types

3.3 Exploring Different Data Types

All the variables contain a data type, it will gain type while you assign value to it, there are 3 basic data types in Python, they are Strings, Numbers, and Booleans.

Strings

It stores text value, it must be within double quotes or single quotes, such as "Hello" or 'How are you?'.

P_03_03_001.py

```
BookName = "Coding Buddies A Simple Journey into Python"
print(BookName)
```

Output

```
Coding Buddies A Simple Journey into Python
```

"BookName" is the variable that stores the Strings data type.

3 Variables and Data Types

If you what to assign multiple lines, you can use 3 double quotes or 3 single quotes.

P_03_03_002.py

```
BookName = """Coding Buddies
A Simple Journey into Python
line 1
line 2
line 3"""
print(BookName)
```

Output

```
Coding Buddies
A Simple Journey into Python
line 1
line 2
line 3
```

3 Variables and Data Types

Numbers

It stores number values which can be integers or floats.

P_03_03_003.py

```
Year = 2023
print(Year)

pi = 3.14
print(pi)
```

Output

```
2023
3.14
```

Booleans

It stores True or False which is commonly used with other logic operators.

P_03_03_004.py

```
IsPythonGood = True
print(IsPythonGood)

IsSunCold = False
print(IsSunCold)
```

Output

```
True
False
```

3 Variables and Data Types

3.4 Understanding Lists

A list is a group of values, indicated by [ ].

For example, this is a List of Numbers.

> [1,2,3,4,5]

For example, this is a List for String.

> ["Tom","Sam","Mary","May","Amy"]

A list can be assigned to a variable.

> CustomerName = ["Tom","Sam","Mary","May","Amy"]

[ ] is used to get or assigned the value in the List, the index is started by 0.

> CustomerName[0] = "Tom"

3 Variables and Data Types

You can get the value by the index inside [ ].

P_03_04_001.py

```
CustomerName = ["Tom","Sam","Mary"]

print( CustomerName[0] )
print( CustomerName[1] )
print( CustomerName[2] )
```

Output

```
Tom
Sam
Mary
```

You can assign a value by the index inside [ ].

P_03_04_002.py

```
CustomerName = ["Tom","Sam","Mary"]
CustomerName[0] = "Paul"

print( CustomerName[0] )
print( CustomerName[1] )
print( CustomerName[2] )
```

Output

```
Paul
Sam
Mary
```

Chapter 4
Comments and Operators

4 Comments and Operators

4.1 Understanding Comments

Comments are not operators, but they are very important, those are the messages between programmers, the code with comments will not be executed, comments play a vital role in making your code more readable, maintainable, and collaborative.

Line Comments

A hash symbol is used for line comments.

P_04_01_001.py

```
# BookName is the variable for the name of the book
BookName = "Coding Buddies A Simple Journey into Python"
print(BookName)
```

Output

```
Coding Buddies A Simple Journey into Python
```

VS code

```
1    # BookName is the variable for name of the book
2    BookName = "Coding Buddies A Simple Journey into Python"
3    print(BookName)
4
```

4 Comments and Operators

Block Comments

3 double quotes or 3 single quotes symbol is used for block comments.

P_04_01_002.py
```
"""
Here is the flow of the program
Step 1 : Assign the variable
Step 2 : output the variable for checking
"""
BookName = "Coding Buddies A Simple Journey into Python"
print(BookName)
```

Output
```
Coding Buddies A Simple Journey into Python
```

VS code
```
1    """
2    Here is the flow of the program
3    Step 1 : Assign the variable
4    Step 2 : output the variable for checking
5    """
6    BookName = "Coding Buddies A Simple Journey into Python"
7    print(BookName)
8
```

 Notes
- You can choose which one suits your need.

4.2 Understanding Operators

Get ready to wield your programming superpowers with Python operators! These handy tools allow you to perform all sorts of amazing feats on your code. With operators, you can...

- Add, subtract, multiply, and divide numbers.
- Concatenate and manipulate text.
- Compare values to make decisions.

And so much more, we will go through some common operators in this section.

4 Comments and Operators

4.3 Arithmetic Operators

+

Add the values together, which can be Strings or Numbers, the + operator is used.

P_04_03_001.py

```
print( 1 + 3 )
print( 'The book name is ' + 'Coding Buddies A Simple Journey into Python' )
```

Output

```
4
The book name is Coding Buddies A Simple Journey into Python
```

 Notes
- For Numbers, the values will be added up.
- For Strings, the values will be concatenate.

4 Comments and Operators

-

Subtract the values, which can be Numbers only, the - operator is used.

P_04_03_002.py
```
print( 3 - 1 )
```

Output
```
2
```

*

Multiply the values, which can be Numbers only, the * sign is used.

P_04_03_003.py
```
print( 3 * 2 )
```

Output
```
6
```

4 Comments and Operators

/

Divide the values, which can be Numbers only, / sign is used.

P_04_03_004.py
```
print( 3 / 2 )
```

Output
```
1.5
```

%

Get the modulus value after dividing the values, which can be Numbers only, the % sign is used.

P_04_03_005.py
```
print( 7 % 2 )
```

Output
```
1
```

4 Comments and Operators

**

Get the power of the values, which can be Numbers only, the ** sign is used.

P_04_03_006.py
```
print( 2 ** 4 )    # same as 2*2*2*2
```

Output
```
16
```

//

Divide the values, and remove the decimal, can be Numbers only, // sign is used.

P_04_03_007.py
```
print( 3 // 2 )
```

Output
```
1
```

4.4 Assignment Operators

=

The operator is used by variables assignment, there are a few different ways to do it, which can be Strings or Numbers.

P_04_04_001.py

```
NumberOfApple = 10
print(NumberOfApple)


NameOFBook = 'Coding Buddies A Simple Journey into Python'
print(NameOFBook)


Str1 = Str2 = Str3 = 'StrX are all the same'
print(Str1)
print(Str2)
print(Str3)
```

Output

```
10
Coding Buddies A Simple Journey into Python
StrX are all the same
StrX are all the same
StrX are all the same
```

4 Comments and Operators

+=

The operator is used for variables assignment, it combines the + and =, which can be Strings or Numbers.

`A = A + 3` same as `A += 3`

P_04_04_002.py

```
NumberOfApple = 10
NumberOfApple += 3
print(NumberOfApple)

NameOFBook = 'Coding Buddies'
NameOFBook += ' A Simple Journey into Python'
print(NameOFBook)
```

Output

```
13
Coding Buddies A Simple Journey into Python
```

4 Comments and Operators

-=

The operator is used for variables assignment, it combines the - and =, which can be Numbers.

`A = A - 3` same as `A -= 3`

P_04_04_003.py

```
NumberOfApple = 10
NumberOfApple -= 3
print(NumberOfApple)
```

Output

```
7
```

*=

The operator is used for variables assignment, it combines the * and =, which can be Numbers.

`A = A * 3` same as `A *= 3`

P_04_04_004.py

```
NumberOfApple = 5
NumberOfApple *= 3
print(NumberOfApple)
```

Output

```
15
```

4 Comments and Operators

/=

The operator is used for variables assignment, it combines the / and =, which can be Numbers.

`A = A / 2` same as `A /= 2`

P_04_04_005.py

```
NumberOfApple = 5
NumberOfApple /= 2
print(NumberOfApple)
```

Output

```
2.5
```

%=

The operator is used for variables assignment, it combines the % and =, which can be Numbers.

`A = A % 3` same as `A %= 3`

P_04_04_006.py

```
NumberOfApple = 10
NumberOfApple %= 3
print(NumberOfApple)
```

Output

```
1
```

//=

The operator is used for variables assignment, it combines the // and =, which can be Numbers.

`A = A // 3` same as `A //= 3`

P_04_04_007.py

```
NumberOfApple = 10
NumberOfApple //= 3
print(NumberOfApple)
```

Output

```
3
```

4 Comments and Operators

4.5 Comparison Operators

They are used to compare 2 values, the result will be a Boolean, which can be True or False.

==

Compare 2 values.

- Return True if they are the same.
- Return False if they are not the same.
- Can be Strings or Numbers.
- == is used.

P_04_05_001.py

```
print( 3 == 3 )
print( 5 == 3 )

print( "One" == "One" )
print( "One" == "Two" )

NumberOfApple = 10
print(NumberOfApple == 10)
print(NumberOfApple == 20)
```

Output

```
True
False
True
False
True
False
```

4 Comments and Operators

!=

Compare 2 values.

- Return True if they are not the same.
- Return False if they are the same.
- Can be Strings or Numbers.
- != is used.

P_04_05_002.py

```
print( 3 != 3 )
print( 5 != 3 )

print( "One" != "One" )
print( "One" != "Two" )

NumberOfApple = 10
print(NumberOfApple != 10)
print(NumberOfApple != 20)
```

Output

```
False
True
False
True
False
True
```

4 Comments and Operators

>

Compare 2 values.

- Return True if the left one is greater than the right one.
- Return False if the left one is not greater than the right one.
- Alphanumerical order used for Strings, e.g. C is greater than A.
- For Strings, it will compare the letters one by one, and move to the next one if the first letter is the same.
- > is used.

P_04_05_003.py

```
print( 3 > 3 )
print( 5 > 3 )
print( 3 > 5 )

print( "A" > "A" )
print( "A" > "C" )
print( "C" > "A" )

print( "ABC" > "AAA" )
```

Output

```
False
True
False
False
False
True
True
```

 Notes

- The comparison of String is using the ASCII table, there has a number of each character, can find the details in Appendix-ACSII Code Table.

4 Comments and Operators

<

Compare 2 values.

- Return True if the left one is less than the right one.
- Return False if the left one is not less than the right one.
- Alphanumerical order used for Strings, e.g. A is less than C.
- For Strings, it will compare the letter one by one, and move to the next one if the first letter is the same.
- < is used.

P_04_05_004.py
```
print( 3 < 3 )
print( 5 < 3 )
print( 3 < 5 )

print( "A" < "A" )
print( "A" < "C" )
print( "C" < "A" )

print( "ABC" < "AAA" )
```

Output
```
False
False
True
False
True
False
False
```

4 Comments and Operators

>=

Compare 2 values.

- Return True if the left one is greater than or equal to the right one.
- Return False if the left one is not greater than or equal to the right one.
- Alphanumerical order used for Strings, e.g. C is greater than A.
- For Strings, it will compare the letters one by one, and move to the next one if the first letter is the same.
- >= is used.

P_04_05_005.py

```
print( 3 >= 3 )
print( 5 >= 3 )
print( 3 >= 5 )

print( "A" >= "A" )
print( "A" >= "C" )
print( "C" >= "A" )

print( "ABC" >= "AAA" )
```

Output

```
True
True
False
True
False
True
True
```

4 Comments and Operators

<=

Compare 2 values.

- Return True if the left one is less than or equal to the right one.
- Return False if the left one is not less than or equal to the right one.
- Alphanumerical order used for Strings, e.g. A is less than C.
- For Strings, it will compare the letter one by one, and move to the next one if the first letter is the same.
- <= is used.

P_04_05_006.py

```
print( 3 <= 3 )
print( 5 <= 3 )
print( 3 <= 5 )

print( "A" <= "A" )
print( "A" <= "C" )
print( "C" <= "A" )

print( "ABC" <= "AAA" )
```

Output

```
True
False
True
True
True
False
False
```

4 Comments and Operators

4.6 Logical Operators

They are used between 2 Boolean.
- The result can be True or False.
- The process order of the logical operator is "not" then "and" then "or".

> not → and → or

- Can use ( ) to indicate which logic goes first.

4 Comments and Operators

and

It processes between 2 Boolean.

- Return True if both of them are True.
- Return False if one of them is False.

P_04_06_001.py

```
print( True and True )
print( True and False )

print( 3>1 and 4>2 )
print( 3>1 and 1>2 )

NumberOfApple = 10
print( NumberOfApple > 5 and NumberOfApple < 20 )
```

Output

```
True
False
True
False
True
```

or

It processes between 2 Boolean.

- Return True if one of them is True.
- Return False if none of them is True.

P_04_06_002.py

```
print( True or True )
print( True or False )
print( False or False )

print( 3>1 or 4>2 )
print( 3>1 or 1>2 )
print( 3>5 or 1>2 )

NumberOfApple = 10
print( NumberOfApple > 5 or NumberOfApple < 20 )
```

Output

```
True
True
False
True
True
False
True
```

4 Comments and Operators

not

it processes for 1 Boolean.

- Return True if it is False.
- Return False if it is True.
- Can use ( ) for more easy to read.

P_04_06_003.py

```
print( not(True) )
print( not True )

print( not(False) )
print( not False )

NumberOfApple = 10
print( not( NumberOfApple > 5 ) )
```

Output

```
False
False
True
True
False
```

Logical Operator Ordering

The process order of the logical operator is "not" then "and" then "or".

not → and → or

Example 1:

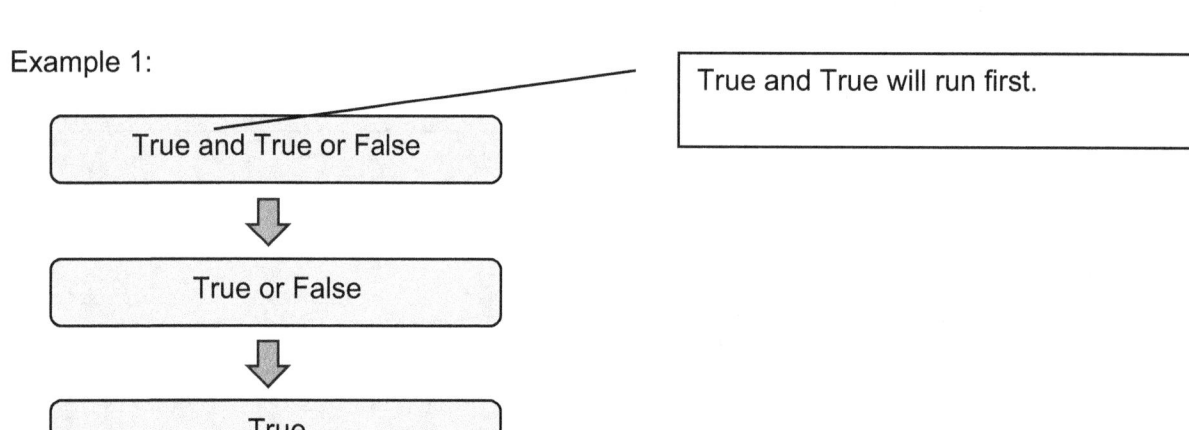

True and True will run first.

Example 2:

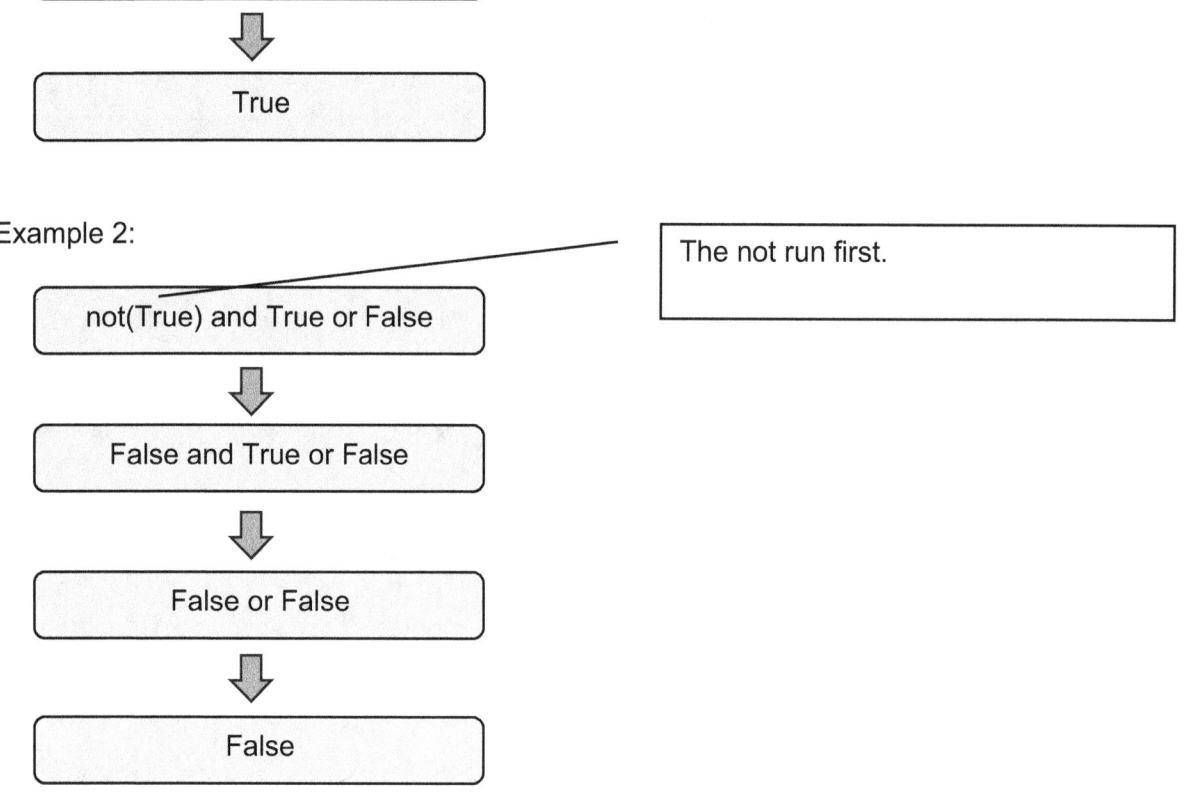

The not run first.

4.7 Identity Operators

Identity operators are to compare the identity of two objects, not the value of the object, objects can be variables or direct values.

is

it processes between 2 objects.
- Return True if they have the same identity.
- Return False if they have a different identity.

Sample 1

In this case, both Number1 and Number2 have the same value but a different identity.

P_04_07_001.py

```
Number1 = 1000
Number2 = 2000 / 2
print( Number1 == Number2 )
print( Number1 is Number2 )
```

Output

```
True
False
```

4 Comments and Operators

Sample 2

In this case, both Number1 and Number2 have the same value and identity because we use Number2 = Number1.

P_04_07_002.py

```
Number1 = 1000
Number2 = Number1
print( Number1 == Number2 )
print( Number1 is Number2 )
```

Output

```
True
True
```

4 Comments and Operators

is not

it processes between 2 objects.

- Return True if they have a different identity.
- Return False if they have the same identity.

P_04_07_003.py

```
Number1 = 1000
Number2 = 2000 / 2
print( Number1 != Number2 )
print( Number1 is not Number2 )
```

Output

```
False
True
```

 Notes

- In most of the time, we care about value, not identity, so == and != are common used.

4.8 Membership Operators

Membership operators are used to check if the value is presented in another object.

in

it processes between 2 objects.

- Return True if find the value.
- Return False if cannot find the value.

P_04_08_001.py

```
print( 'book' in 'This is a book.' )
print( 'phone' in 'This is a book.' )
```

Output

```
True
False
```

4 Comments and Operators

not in

it processes between 2 objects.

- Return True if cannot find the value.
- Return False if find the value.

P_04_08_002.py

```
print( 'book' not in 'This is a book.' )
print( 'phone' not in 'This is a book.' )
```

Output

```
False
True
```

Chapter 5
Control Flow and Decision Making

5 Control Flow and Decision Making

5.1 Understanding the Control Flow

In the world of programming, conditional constructs are the code that enables your code to make decisions and take different paths based on specific conditions.

For example, you need to send an alert if you have less than 5 apples, here is the flow.

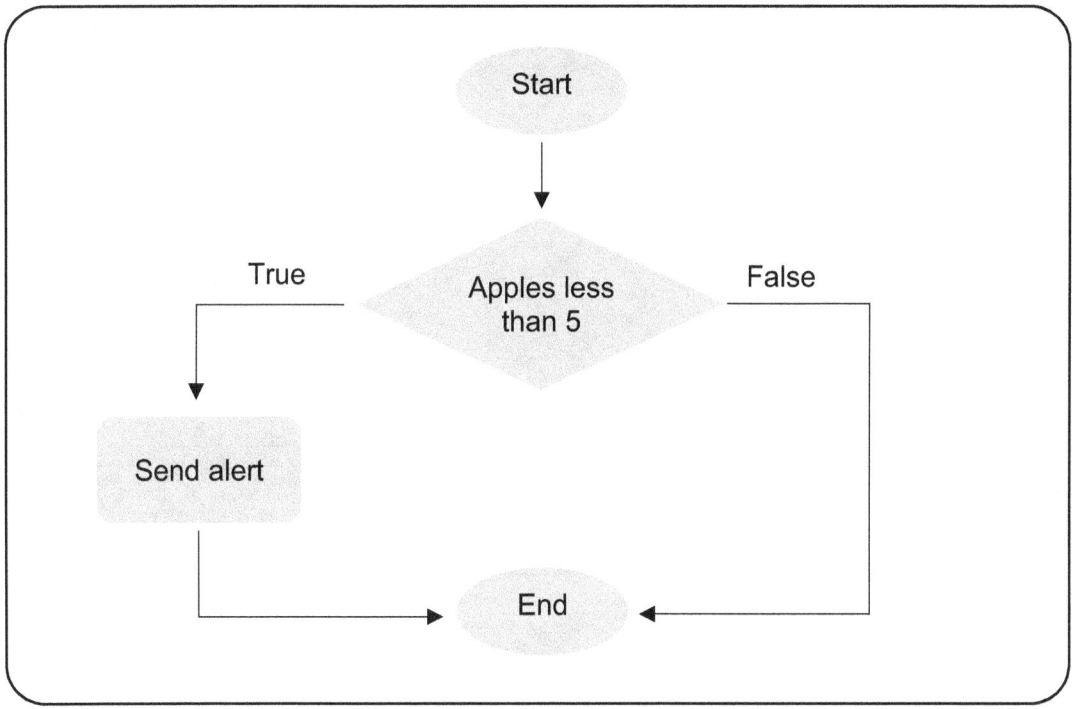

In this case, you need the decision-making code to control the flow, conditional and looping constructs are the code you need for that task.

5 Control Flow and Decision Making

5.2 Conditional

If

The "if" is used to control the logic flow.

- Run the code if the condition is True.
- Skip the code if the condition is False.

P_05_02_001.py

```
NumberOfApple = 3

if (NumberOfApple < 5) :
    print('Send the alert..')
    print('Apple needed.')
```

Output

```
Send the alert..
Apple needed.
```

```
if (NumberOfApple < 5) :
    print('Send the alert..')
    print(Apple needed.')
```

The : is used for the ending of condition.

5 Control Flow and Decision Making

The indentation is to indicate they are under same "if" block.

```
if (NumberOfApple < 5) :
    print('Send the alert..')
    print(Apple needed.')
```

If we remove the indentation, it will not belong to that "if" block.

```
if (NumberOfApple < 5) :
    print('Send the alert..')
print(Apple needed.')
```

In this sample, "Check Done" will be shown.

P_05_02_002.py

```
NumberOfApple = 10

if (NumberOfApple < 5) :
    print('Send the alert..')
print('Checking Done')
```

Output

```
Checking Done
```

 Notes

- The space is very important in Python, it indicate which block that the code belong to.

Page 83

5 Control Flow and Decision Making

If else

The "if else" is used to control the logic flow.

- Run the first part of the code if the condition is True.
- Run the second part of the code if the condition is False.

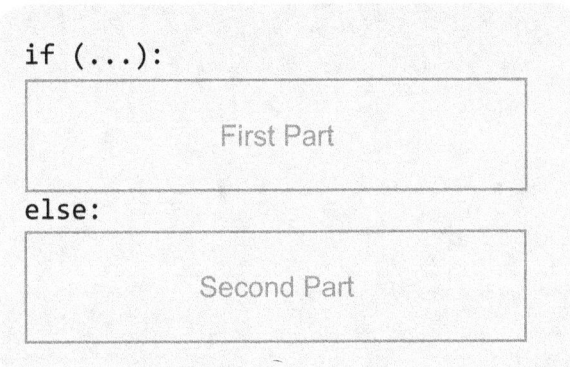

P_05_02_003.py

```
NumberOfApple = 10

if (NumberOfApple < 5) :
    print('Send the alert..')
else:
    print('Apple ok...')
print('Checking Done')
```

Output

```
Apple ok...
Checking Done
```

5 Control Flow and Decision Making

If elif else

The "if elif else" is used to control the logic flow.

- It will test the logic one by one, and run the code that first got the True value.
- You can use the "elif" more than one time.

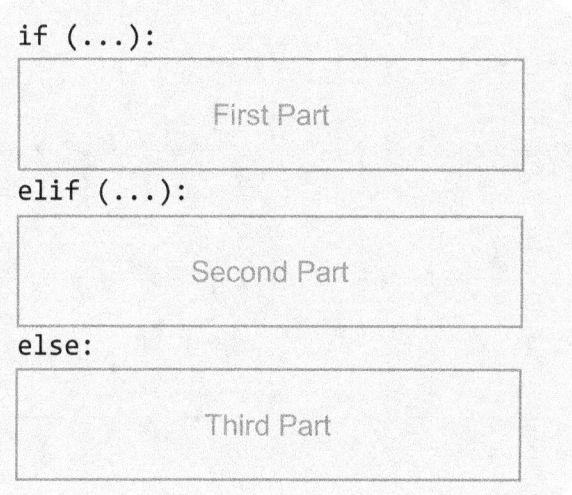

P_05_02_004.py

```
NumberOfApple = 1

if (NumberOfApple < 3) :
    print('Send the alert with urgent!!')
elif (NumberOfApple < 10):
    print('Send the alert..')
else:
    print('Apple ok...')
print('Checking Done')
```

Output

```
Send the alert with urgent!!
Checking Done
```

5 Control Flow and Decision Making

P_05_02_005.py

```
NumberOfApple = 5

if (NumberOfApple < 3) :
    print('Send the alert with urgent!!')
elif (NumberOfApple < 10):
    print('Send the alert..')
else:
    print('Apple ok...')
print('Checking Done')
```

Output

```
Send the alert..
Checking Done
```

P_05_02_006.py

```
NumberOfApple = 15

if (NumberOfApple < 3) :
    print('Send the alert with urgent!!')
elif (NumberOfApple < 10):
    print('Send the alert..')
else:
    print('Apple ok...')
print('Checking Done')
```

Output

```
Apple ok...
Checking Done
```

5 Control Flow and Decision Making

5.3 Looping

If you need to repeat some steps until the requirement is met, looping will be needed.

For example, you need to pick 5 apples, you will need a loop to do that.

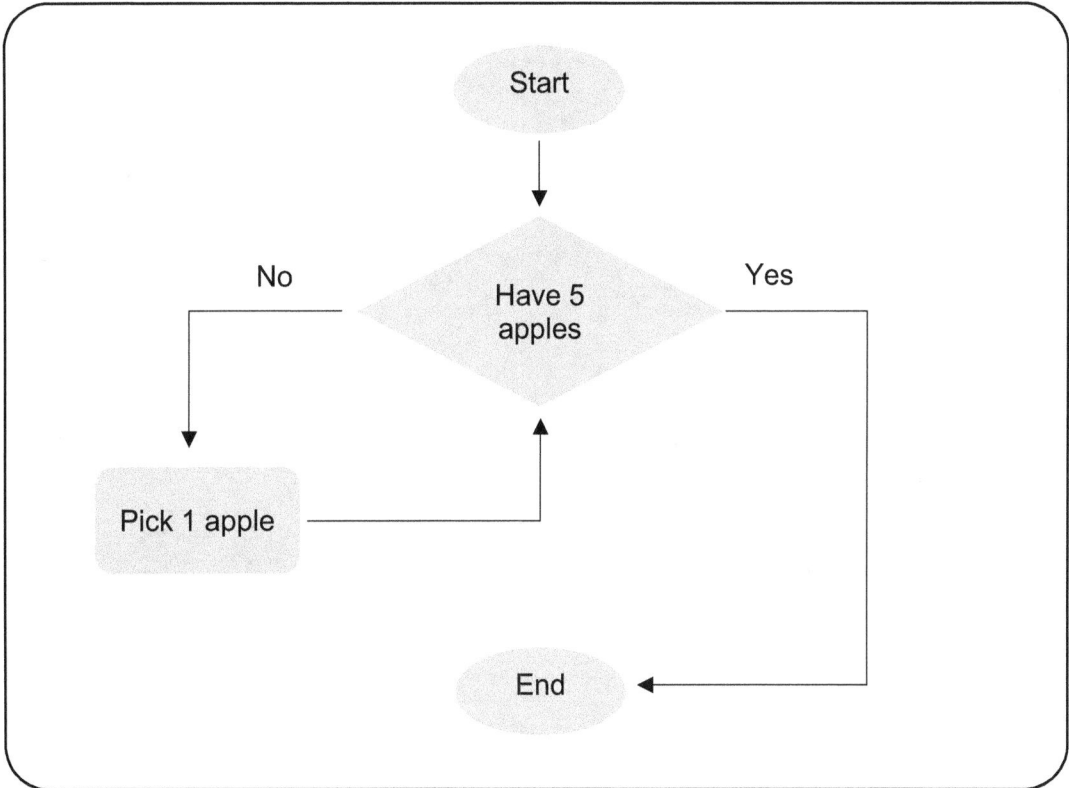

5 Control Flow and Decision Making

while

The "while" is used to loop the code until the requirement is met.

- Repeat until the requirement is met.
- Go back to validate the condition after the last line of the code.

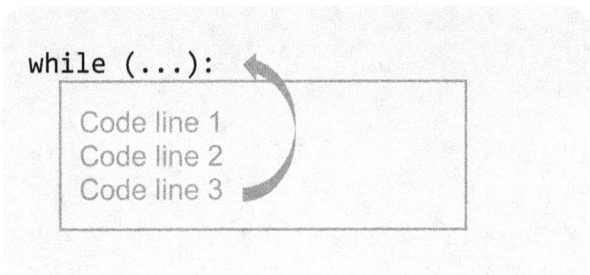

P_05_03_001.py

```
NumberOfApple = 0

while (NumberOfApple<5):
    print('Pick 1 apple..')
    NumberOfApple += 1
print(NumberOfApple)
```

Output

```
Pick 1 apple..
Pick 1 apple..
Pick 1 apple..
Pick 1 apple..
Pick 1 apple..
5
```

5 Control Flow and Decision Making

for

The "for" is used to loop the code for each value.

- A variable will be created.
- Repeat until done for each value.

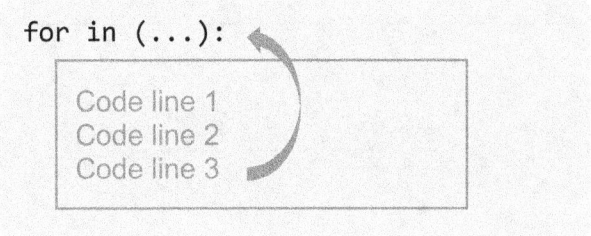

P_05_03_002.py

```
ListOfApple=[1,2,3,4,5]
for NumberOfApple in ListOfApple:
    print(NumberOfApple)
print(NumberOfApple)
```

Output

```
1
2
3
4
5
5
```

break

The "break" is used when you want to terminate the loop.

For example, you want to count the apple until 3.

P_05_03_003.py

```
ListOfApple=[1,2,3,4,5]

for NumberOfApple in ListOfApple:
    print(NumberOfApple)
    if (NumberOfApple==3):
        break


print('---- final value----')
print(NumberOfApple)
```

Output

```
1
2
3
---- final value----
3
```

continue

The "continue" is used when you want to skip one of the values in the loop, it will go back to the beginning of for and assign the next value to the variable.

For example, you want to skip the count of 3.

P_05_03_004.py

```
ListOfApple=[1,2,3,4,5]

for NumberOfApple in ListOfApple:
    if (NumberOfApple==3):
        continue
    print(NumberOfApple)


print('---- final value----')
print(NumberOfApple)
```

Output

```
1
2
4
5
---- final value----
5
```

Chapter 6
Functions and Modules

6 Functions and Modules

6.1 Understanding Functions

Functions are reusable blocks of code that perform specific tasks, making your code modular, efficient, and organized.

The simple format of a function is a function name, and the ( ).

> FunctionName()

Parameters can be used inside the ( ), they are the values that pass into the function.

> FunctionName(1 , 2)

The "print" is the function that we used a lot in the previous session, it will output the values to the terminal.

P_06_01_001.py

```
print("This is a function.")
```

Output

```
This is a function.
```

6 Functions and Modules

Functions can return value to a variable.

> Variable1 = FunctionName(1 , 2)

For example, we use a " max " function to find the biggest values.

P_06_01_002.py

```
MaxValue = max(1,2,4,5,3)
print( MaxValue )
```

Output

```
5
```

 Notes
- The "max" is one of the build-in function in Python, will go to details in next section.

6 Functions and Modules

6.2 Exploring Common Functions

Python comes with a wide range of ready-to-use functionalities, and these functions can help you perform tasks easily.

We will go through some common functions, the full list can be found here:
https://docs.python.org/3/library/functions.html

abs

The "abs" returns the absolute value of a number.

abs(*number*)

Parameter	Description	Required	Default
number	The number value.	Yes	

P_06_02_abs.py

```
result = abs(-32)
print( result )
```

Output
```
32
```

6 Functions and Modules

round

The "round" returns the rounded value of a number.

round(*number, digits*)

Parameter	Description	Required	Default
number	The number value.	Yes	
digits	Round to how many digits?	No	0

P_06_02_round.py

```
result = round(1.555)
print( result )

result = round(1.555,1)
print( result )
```

Output

```
2
1.6
```

6 Functions and Modules

str

The "str" returns the string value of a number.

str(*number, encoding, errors*)

Parameter	Description	Required	Default
number	The number value.	Yes	
encoding	The encoding of the result.	No	UTF-8
errors	Specifies what will do if it has an encoding error. ignore / strict	No	

P_06_02_str.py

```
result = str(10)
print( "We have " + result + " apples." )
```

Output

```
We have 10 apples.
```

 Notes
- In most of the time, we only use the number parameter.
- We need to convert Numbers to Strings, then do the concatenate Stings.

max

The "max" returns the biggest value from the List.

```
max( list )
```

Parameter	Description	Required	Default
list	The list of values.	Yes	

P_06_02_max.py

```
ListOfValues = [4,5,4.3,6]
MaxValue = max(ListOfValues)
print(MaxValue )

ListOfValues = ["apple","may","June"]
MaxValue = max(ListOfValues)
print(MaxValue )
```

Output

```
6
May
```

min

The "min" returns the smallest value from the List.

min(*list*)

Parameter	Description	Required	Default
list	The list of values.	Yes	

P_06_02_min.py

```
ListOfValues = [4,5,4.3,6]
MinValue = min(ListOfValues)
print(MinValue )

ListOfValues = ["apple","may","June"]
MinValue = min(ListOfValues)
print(MinValue )
```

Output

```
4
June
```

6 Functions and Modules

range

The "range" is an immutable sequence type, like a List, which can call as below.

> range(*stop*)

Parameter	Description	Required	Default
stop	The count will start from 0, and add 1 each time until reach the stop parameter.	Yes	

P_06_02_range_001.py

```
for NumberOfApple in range(3):
    print(NumberOfApple)
```

Output

```
0
1
2
```

6 Functions and Modules

> range(*start*, *stop, step*)

Parameter	Description	Required	Default
start	The start number value.	Yes	
stop	Stop when reach the stop number value.	Yes	
step	The increased value for each step.	No	1

P_06_02_range_002.py

```
for NumberOfApple in range(2,10,2):
    print(NumberOfApple)
```

Output

```
2
4
6
8
```

6 Functions and Modules

len

The "len" return the size of the Strings or Lists.

> len(*object*)

Parameter	Description	Required	Default
object	The object that needs to find the length.	Yes	

P_06_02_len.py

```
Name = "Mary"
print( len(Name) )

ListOfName = ["King","Mary","Sam","May","Tom"]
print( len(ListOfName) )
```

Output

```
4
5
```

upper

The "upper" return the upper case of the Strings.

> *strings*.upper()

Parameter	Description	Required	Default
strings	The strings that need to change.	Yes	

P_06_02_upper.py

```
Name = "Mary"
print(  Name.upper()  )
```

Output

```
MARY
```

 Notes
- It is a function from Strings, so we use .upper().

6 Functions and Modules

lower

The "lower" return the lowercase of the Strings.

strings.lower()

Parameter	Description	Required	Default
strings	The strings that need to change.	Yes	

P_06_02_lower.py

```
Name = "Mary"
print(   Name.lower()   )
```

Output

```
Mary
```

6 Functions and Modules

replace

The "replace" returns the Strings that replace the old Strings with the new ones.

> *strings*.replace(*old, new*)

Parameter	Description	Required	Default
strings	The strings that need to change.	Yes	
old	The old strings need to replace.	Yes	
new	The new strings that need to be.	Yes	

P_06_02_replace.py

```
SendOutMessage = "I want to eat apples."
print( SendOutMessage.replace("apples","banana") )
```

Output

```
I want to eat banana.
```

split

The "split" return a List that split the Strings by a character.

> *strings*.split(*char*)

Parameter	Description	Required	Default
strings	The strings that need to split.	Yes	
char	The separator.	No	Space

P_06_02_split.py

```
SendOutMessage = "I want to eat apples."
print(   SendOutMessage.split()   )
```

Output

```
['I', 'want', 'to', 'eat', 'apples.']
```

strip

The "strip" return Strings that remove the space both at the left and right.

> *strings*.strip()

Parameter	Description	Required	Default
strings	The strings need to remove space.	Yes	

P_06_02_strip.py

```
SendOutMessage = "   I want to eat apples.    "
print(  SendOutMessage.strip()  )
```

Output

```
I want to eat apples.
```

6 Functions and Modules

format

The "format" return the converted value.

format(*value*, *option*)

Parameter	Description	Required	Default
value	The value that you want to convert.	Yes	
option	For the format that you what to be, can see the Appendix – Format Option for details.	Yes	

P_06_02_format.py

```
print(   format(1234567,",") )
```

Output

```
1,234,567
```

6 Functions and Modules

6.3 Creating New Functions

Besides the building function, you can also create a function on your own.
- "def" is used for creating a new function.
- Can use Parmenter.
- Can return value.

The simple way of a function can be looks like this.

```
def FunctionName():
    print('This a function')
```

When you use it, you can directly use the function name.

```
FunctionName()
```

P_06_03_001.py

```
def PrintAlert():
    print('Alert:')

PrintAlert()
```

Output

```
Alert:
```

6 Functions and Modules

You can add Parmenter to the function.

The simple way of a function can be looks like this.

```
def FunctionName( Var ):
    print(Var)
```

This is the Parmenter, it will become the Variables in that function.

P_06_03_002.py

```
def PrintAlert(str):
    print('Alert:' + str)

PrintAlert('This is the first error...')
PrintAlert('This is the second error...')
```

Output

```
Alert:This is the first error...
Alert:This is the second error...
```

6 Functions and Modules

You can use 'return' to the function, the function will return the value.

P_06_03_003.py

```
def isLessThen5(Number):
    if Number<5:
        return True
    else:
        return False

print( isLessThen5(1) )
print( isLessThen5(10) )
```

Output

```
True
False
```

 Notes
- The 'return' will also end the function, code after return will not be executed.

6 Functions and Modules

6.4 Organizing With Modules

Modules help to group the functions into a package so that we can reuse them more easily.

For example, this module file contains the function we created before.

myModule.py

```
def PrintAlert(str):
    print('Alert:' + str)

def isLessThen5(Number):
    if Number<5:
        return True
    else:
        return False
```

Use 'import' to link the myModule.py, so don't have to create the function again.

P_06_04_001.py

```
import myModule

myModule.PrintAlert('This is the first error...')
myModule.PrintAlert('This is the second error...')
print( myModule.isLessThen5(1) )
print( myModule.isLessThen5(10) )
```

Output

```
Alert:This is the first error...
Alert:This is the second error...
True
False
```

6 Functions and Modules

Use 'import … as …' to shorten the name.

P_06_04_002.py

```
import myModule as my

my.PrintAlert('This is the first error...')
my.PrintAlert('This is the second error...')
print( my.isLessThen5(1) )
print( my.isLessThen5(10) )
```

Output

```
Alert:This is the first error...
Alert:This is the second error...
True
False
```

Use 'from … import …' to link the myModule.py, so don't have to mention the module name every time.

P_06_04_003.py

```
from myModule import PrintAlert,isLessThen5

PrintAlert('This is the first error...')
PrintAlert('This is the second error...')
print( isLessThen5(1) )
print( isLessThen5(10) )
```

Output

```
Alert:This is the first error...
Alert:This is the second error...
True
False
```

6 Functions and Modules

6.5 Exploring Built-in Modules

Python had some built-in Modules that we can use, here are some common Modules that we use.

datetime

This module handles the date or date time for Python, it has a lot of functions to use, here are some samples.

Use 'datetime.datetime.now()' to get the current date time.

P_06_05_001.py

```
import datetime

CurrentTime = datetime.datetime.now()
print(CurrentTime)
```

Output

```
2023-07-22 23:29:00.332662
```

6 Functions and Modules

Use 'datetime.datetime(year , month, day)' to create a date object.

P_06_05_002.py

```
import datetime
todate = datetime.datetime(2023, 7, 22)
print(todate)
```

Output

```
2023-07-22 00:00:00
```

Use 'weekday()' to get the day of the week as an integer, where Monday is 0 and Sunday is 6

P_06_05_003.py

```
import datetime
todate = datetime.datetime(2023, 7, 22)
print(todate.weekday())
```

Output

```
5
```

 Notes
- Details for datetime can be find in https://docs.python.org/3/library/datetime.html

6 Functions and Modules

math

This module handles the math functions for Python, here are some samples.

Use 'ceil' to return the ceiling of the value.

P_06_05_004.py

```
import math

print( math.ceil(1.1)  )
```

Output

```
2
```

For example, 'floor' returns the floor of the value.

P_06_05_005.py

```
import math

print( math.floor(1.9)  )
```

Output

```
1
```

 Notes
- Details for math can be find in https://docs.python.org/3/library/math.html

Chapter 7
External Modules

7 External Modules

7.1 Understanding External Module

External modules are pre-packaged libraries created by other developers, offering a treasure trove of additional functionalities. These modules extend Python's capabilities, allowing you to tackle a wide range of tasks.

You can find external modules for Python in the Python Package Index (PyPI), which is a repository of Python software packages maintained by the Python community. PyPI hosts a vast collection of external modules, also known as packages, that you can easily install and use in your Python projects, here on the PyPI website.

https://pypi.org/

Besides PyPI, there are tons of organizations that provide free and open-source modules, you can google them.

7 External Modules

7.2 PIP Install

Once you find a Module that you what to use, you have to install it, most likely, you will see something like this.

Install

```
pip install pysimplegui
or
pip3 install pysimplegui
```

The pip or pip3 is the install command, you can go to the Terminal in VS code and type the command.

7 External Modules

The Module will install automatically.

```
Collecting pysimplegui
  Downloading PySimpleGUI-4.60.5-py3-none-any.whl (512 kB)
                                                   512.7/512.7 kB 2.5 MB/s eta 0:00:00
Installing collected packages: pysimplegui
Successfully installed pysimplegui-4.60.4

[notice] A new release of pip is available: 23.0.1 -> 23.2.1
[notice] To update, run: python.exe -m pip install --upgrade pip
```

Then you can use the new Module.

```
1
2    import pysimplegui
3
4
5
6
```

7 External Modules

7.3 Using External Module

Let's use the PySimpleGUI which we installed as a sample, it provides an easy way to create your own Windows interface.

Go to the PySimpleGUI webpage, you can find the overview and installation guide on the home page.

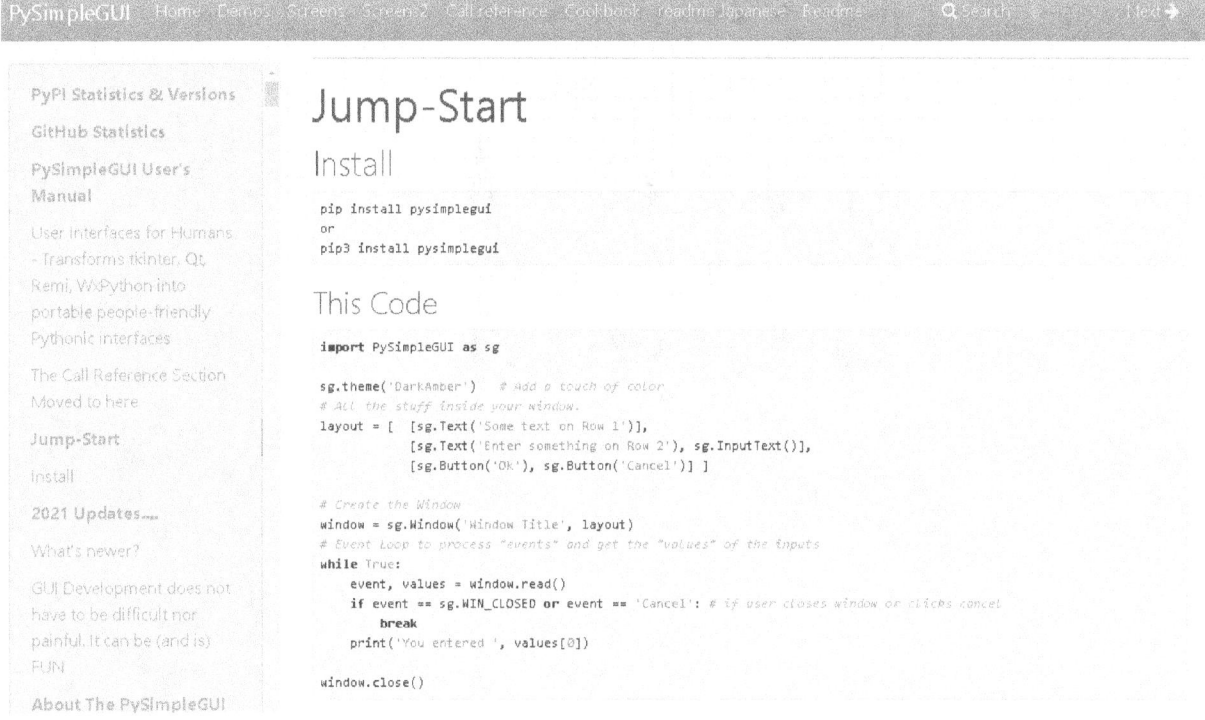

7 External Modules

You can find some demos file in "Demos".

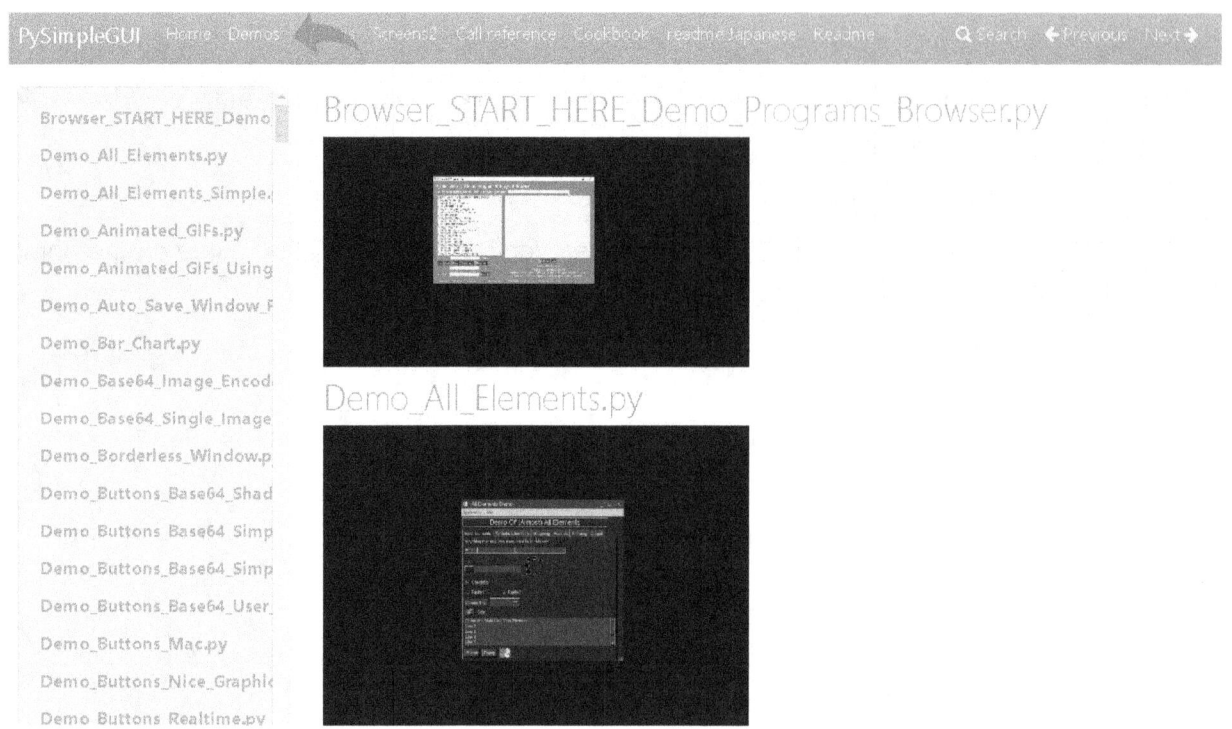

 Notes
- Most of the Module have a demo section, it is a good way to know what it can do.

7 External Modules

You can find the details in the "Call Reference".

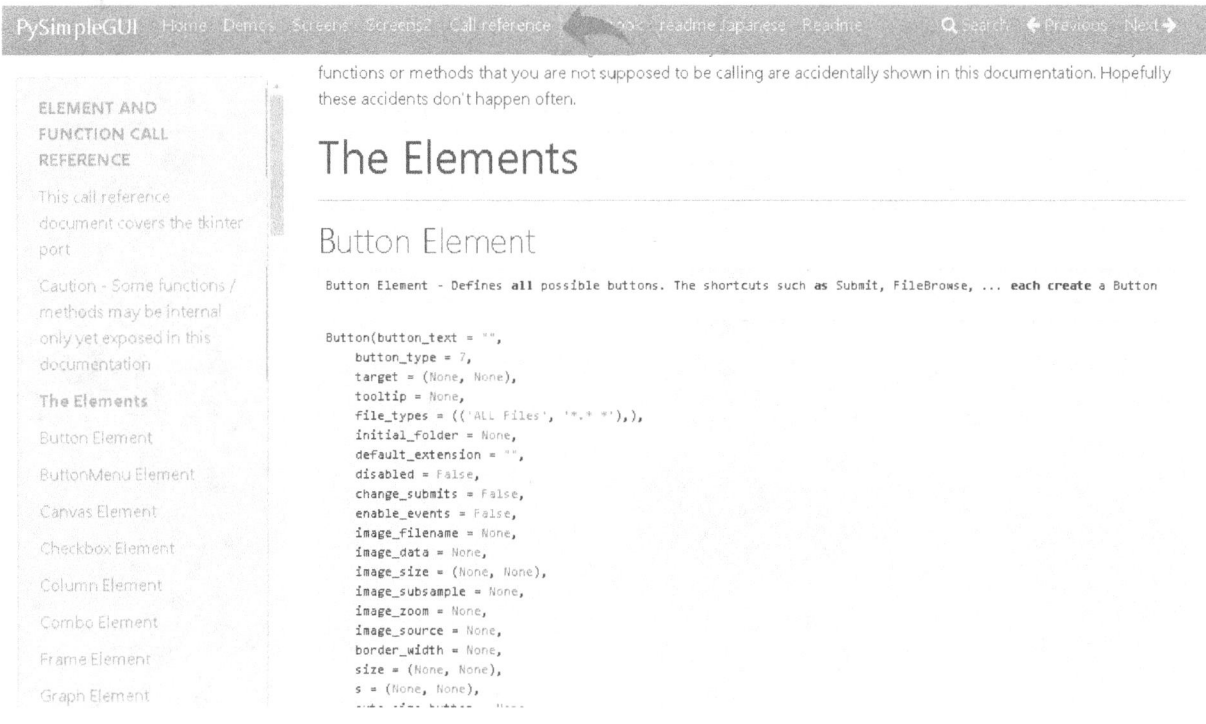

 Notes
- Most of the Module have a reference section, it is a good way to know the details usage.

7 External Modules

Let's try on the quick tour.

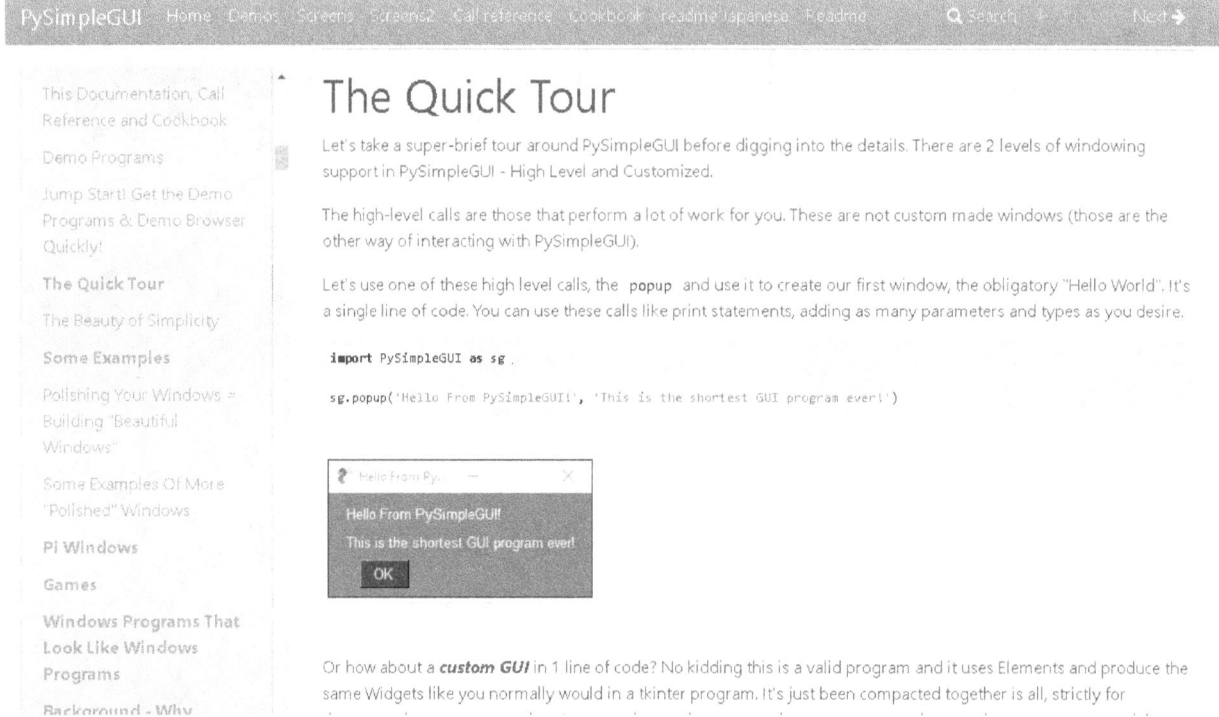

P_07_03_001.py

```
import PySimpleGUI as sg

sg.popup('Hello From PySimpleGUI!', 'This is the shortest GUI program ever!')
```

Output

7 External Modules

The popup() is a function from PySimpleGUI, you can find the details information under "Call reference".

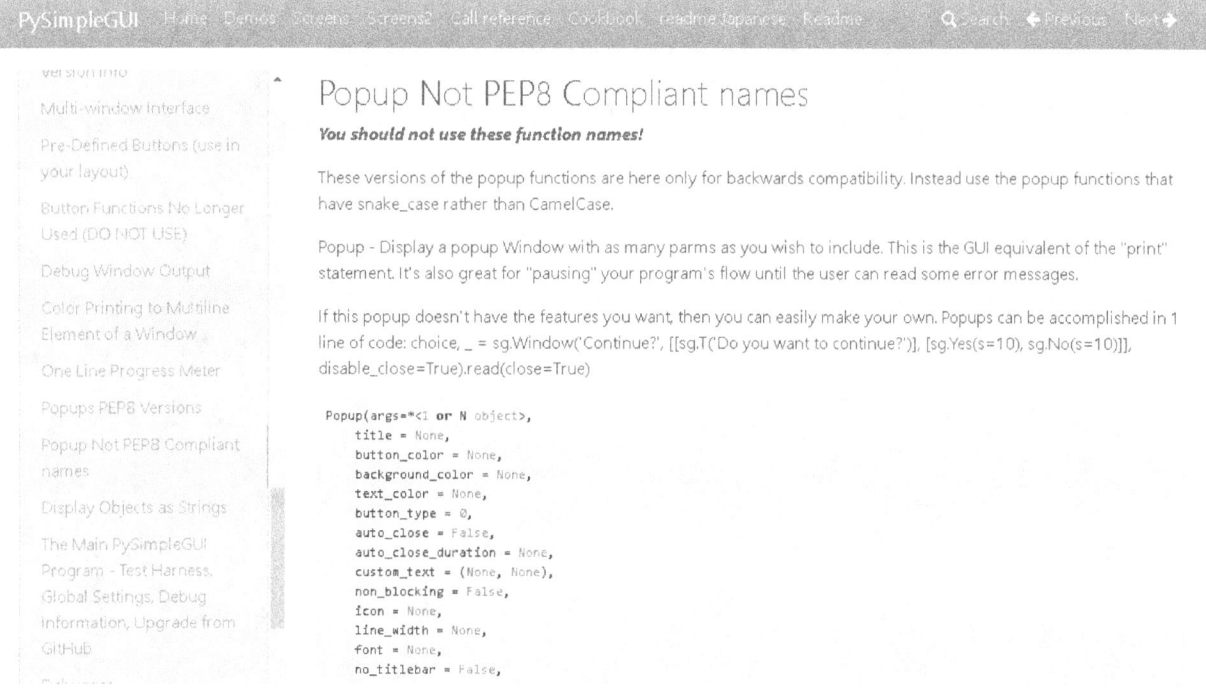

7 External Modules

It shows what you can do with the popup function.

```
Popup(args=*<1 or N object>,
    title = None,
    button_color = None,
    background_color = None,
    text_color = None,
    button_type = 0,
    auto_close = False,
    auto_close_duration = None,
    custom_text = (None, None),
    non_blocking = False,
    icon = None,
    line_width = None,
    font = None,
    no_titlebar = False,
    grab_anywhere = False,
    keep_on_top = None,
    location = (None, None),
    relative_location = (None, None),
    any_key_closes = False,
    image = None,
    modal = True,
    button_justification = None,
    drop_whitespace = True)
```

Let's try on the text_color.

```
Popup(args=*<1 or N object>,
    title = None,
    button_color = None,
    background_color = None,
    text_color = None,
    button_type = 0,
    auto_close = False,
    auto_close_duration = None,
    custom_text = (None, None),
```

7 External Modules

Change the text to another color.

P_07_03_002.py

```
import PySimpleGUI as sg

sg.popup('Hello From PySimpleGUI!', 'This is the shortest GUI program
ever!',text_color='red')
```

Output

Notes

- You can play around with other settings.

7 External Modules

Next, we try on the other one.

The Beauty of Simplicity

One day I will find the right words, and they will be simple. — Jack Kerouac

That's nice that you can crunch things into 1 line, like in the above example, but it's not readable. Let's add some whitespace so you can see the **beauty** of the PySimpleGUI code. And while we're at it, we'll change the color theme to something darker that's perhaps more attractive to some of you.

Take a moment and look at the code below. Can you "see" the window looking at the `layout` variable, knowing that each line of code represents a single row of Elements? There are 3 "rows" of Elements shown in the window and there are 3 lines of code that define it.

Creating and reading the user's inputs for the window occupy the last 2 lines of code, one to create the window, the last line shows the window to the user and gets the input values (what button they clicked, what was input in the Input Element)

```python
import PySimpleGUI as sg

sg.theme('Dark Grey 13')

layout = [[sg.Text('Filename')],
          [sg.Input(), sg.FileBrowse()],
          [sg.OK(), sg.Cancel()]]

window = sg.Window('Get filename example', layout)

event, values = window.read()
window.close()
```

7 External Modules

P_07_03_003.py

```
import PySimpleGUI as sg

sg.theme('Dark Grey 13')

layout = [[sg.Text('Filename')],
          [sg.Input(), sg.FileBrowse()],
          [sg.OK(), sg.Cancel()]]

window = sg.Window('Get filename example', layout)

event, values = window.read()
window.close()
```

Output

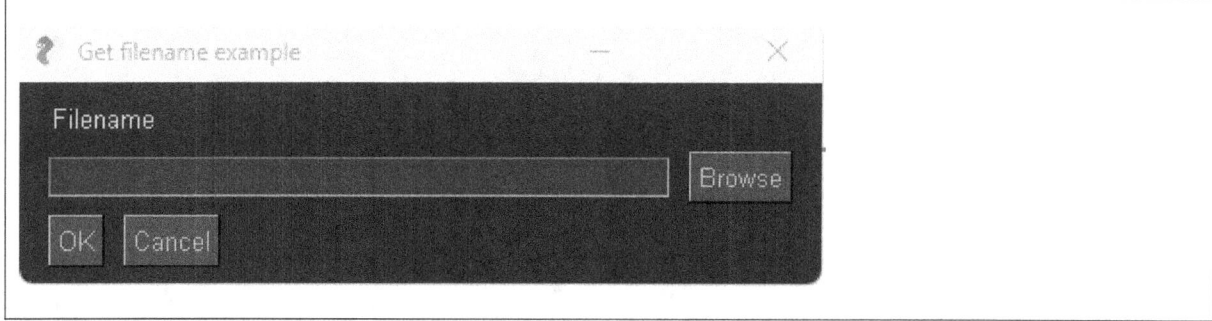

7 External Modules

Explanation

Code	What does it do?
sg.theme('Dark Grey 13')	Set the elements that to match the colors.
sg.Text('Filename')	Create a text.
sg.Input()	Create a text input.
sg.FileBrowse()	Create a file browse button.
sg.OK()	Create a file OK button.
sg.Cancel()	Create a file cancel button.
layout	List of the control objects.
sg.Window()	Create a window, the object based on a List.
window.read()	Start the windows and wait for input.
window.close()	Close the windows.

You can find the details under the "Call Reference".

7 External Modules

This is a sample for handling events.

P_07_03_004.py

```python
import PySimpleGUI as sg

layout = [
            [sg.Input( key='-TxtInput-' )]
            ,[sg.OK( key='-BtnOk-')]
         ]
window = sg.Window('Testing', layout)
event, values = window.read()

if event == '-BtnOk-':
    print( values['-TxtInput-'] )

window.close()
```

Output

Hello

Explanation

Code	What does it do?
sg.Input(key='-TxtInput-')	Create a text input and give it a key, the key is the name of the object.
if event == '-BtnOk-':	Check the event with the key.
values['-TxtInput-']	Get the values of the input by key.

The Last Tips

8 The Last Tips

The world of Python is huge, and it changes rapidly, this book cannot give you every detail in Python, however, it gives you the basic knowledge of Python, and then you can get into it by yourself.

I aim to get you started and give you the skills that you need, you will know how to find updated and advanced technology by yourself.

Tips 1:
Google, pypi.org, and python.org will be your best teacher.

Tips 2:
Most of the External Modules have a "Hello world" demo, start there.

Tips 3:
Always go for "Reference" for detailed information.

Tips 4:
Go to see the demo first if there is one.

Appendix

9 Appendix

9.1 ASCII Code Table

Here is some common character in ASCII (American Standard Code for Information Interchange).

#	Char	#	Char	#	Char	#	Char	#	Char	#	Char
32	Space	52	4	72	H	92	\	112	p		
33	!	53	5	73	I	93	]	113	q		
34	"	54	6	74	J	94	^	114	r		
35	#	55	7	75	K	95	_	115	s		
36	$	56	8	76	L	96	`	116	t		
37	%	57	9	77	M	97	a	117	u		
38	&	58	:	78	N	98	b	118	v		
39	'	59	;	79	O	99	c	119	w		
40	(	60	<	80	P	100	d	120	x		
41	)	61	=	81	Q	101	e	121	y		
42	*	62	>	82	R	102	f	122	z		
43	+	63	?	83	S	103	g	123	{		
44	,	64	@	84	T	104	h	124				
45	-	65	A	85	U	105	i	125	}		
46	.	66	B	86	V	106	j	126	~		
47	/	67	C	87	W	107	k				
48	0	68	D	88	X	108	l				
49	1	69	E	89	Y	109	m				
50	2	70	F	90	Z	110	n				
51	3	71	G	91	[	111	o				

9 Appendix

9.2 Format Option

Here is some common format option for Python.

Option	Meaning
<	Forces the field to be left-aligned within the available space (this is the default for most objects).
>	Forces the field to be right-aligned within the available space (this is the default for numbers).
=	Forces the padding to be placed after the sign (if any) but before the digits. This is used for printing fields in the form '+000000120'. This alignment option is only valid for numeric types. It becomes the default for numbers when '0' immediately precedes the field width.
^	Forces the field to be centered within the available space.
+	Indicates that a sign should be used for both positive as well as negative numbers.
-	Indicates that a sign should be used only for negative numbers (this is the default behavior).
space	Indicates that a leading space should be used on positive numbers and a minus sign on negative numbers.
,	Use a comma as a thousand separator.
_	Use an underscore as a thousand separator.
s	String format. This is the default type for strings and may be omitted.
b	Binary format. Outputs the number in base 2.
d	Decimal Integer. Outputs the number in base 10.
o	Octal format. Outputs the number in base 8.
x	Hex format. Output the number in base 16, using lower-case letters for the digits above 9.
X	Hex format. Output the number in base 16, using upper-case letters for the digits above 9. In case '#' is specified, the prefix '0x' will be upper-cased to '0X' as well.
e	Scientific notation. For a given precision p, formats the number in scientific notation with the letter 'e' separating the coefficient from the exponent. The coefficient has one digit before and p digits after the decimal point, for a total of p + 1 significant digits. With no precision given, uses a precision of 6 digits after the decimal point for float, and shows all coefficient digits for Decimal. If no digits follow the decimal point, the decimal point is also removed unless the # option is used.
f	Fixed-point notation. For a given precision p, formats the number as a decimal number with exactly p digits following the decimal point. With no precision given, uses a precision of 6 digits after the decimal point for float, and uses a precision large enough to show all coefficient digits for Decimal. If no digits follow the decimal point, the decimal point is also removed unless the # option is used.

9 Appendix

%	Percentage. Multiplies the number by 100 and displays in fixed ('f') format, followed by a percent sign.

ABOUT THE AUTHOR

Meet our incredible author, whose passion for programming ignited at the tender age of 10, setting the course for a lifelong journey in the world of technology. With an unwavering interest in programming, they embarked on their path to becoming a software developer, and there was no looking back.

Having dedicated over two decades to the field of software development, our author's expertise has grown immensely, enriched by the experience of being a part of this ever-evolving industry since 2001.

With boundless curiosity and a heart dedicated to fostering a thriving coding community, our author continues to make a significant impact in the tech realm, leaving a trail of innovation and excellence wherever they go.

www.ingramcontent.com/pod-product-compliance
Lightning Source LLC
Chambersburg PA
CBHW082108220526
45472CB00009B/2093